# 'Folk Hero Forever'

## The Eclectic, Enthralling Baseball Life of Luke Easter

Alex Painter

© Alex Painter, 2018

All images courtesy of the Cleveland Indians team archives or belong in the public domain.

This one goes out to 'Big Luke' Easter. I only hope I have done your incredible story justice. The pleasure has been all mine.

## Table of Contents

Preface .......................................................................................... vii
Introduction: A Prodigious Swat ................................................. 13
1. From the Delta to the Gateway City ..................................... 19
2. The Titanium Giants and the Wartime Years ...................... 26
3. Abe Saperstein and the Crescents ........................................ 34
4. 1947: An Heir Apparent Arises, the Color Barrier Falls ......... 40
5. The Negro Leagues ................................................................ 50
6. The Coastal Phenom ............................................................. 59
7. A (Bitter) Cup of Coffee ........................................................ 70
8. Breakout ................................................................................ 79
9. Different Year, Still Chasin' the Yankees ............................. 92
10. Well, I'll be Damned ........................................................... 101
11. On the Outs ......................................................................... 111
12. What Next? .......................................................................... 120
13. International League Royalty ............................................. 125
Conclusion ................................................................................. 137
Appendix A: A Yearly Log of 'Easter Eggs' ................................ 141
Appendix B: That Famous Card Shark Story ........................... 142
Appendix C: The First Dozen: A Timeline of Baseball Integration
.................................................................................................... 144
Bibliography ............................................................................... 145
Index ........................................................................................... 152
Notes .......................................................................................... 159

## Preface

The genesis of "Folk Hero Forever" can be traced to simple curiosity, with a rather unassuming baseball card providing the flashpoint. Like many children of the 1990s, I collected baseball cards. I accumulated them by the thousands. Armed with a couple dollars in my pocket, I would rifle through the dime box at the local card store, until my combination of exactly 20 cards was perfect. Sometimes, this process would take hours. Ultimately, I had assembled a baseball card collection that rivaled, even dwarfed, those of any of my brothers (I have six), the other neighborhood kids, friends, school bullies, the bus driver, you name it. Like many of those diehard, preteen baseball card collectors of the 1990s, there was a hiatus in my status as a collector. However, unlike many of my peers, my hiatus was not indefinite.

Upon graduating from college I catapulted, at breakneck speed, back into collecting baseball cards the summer of 2010. Having a strong history background, and discovering keeping up with all of new baseball cards would be an exhausting endeavor, I decided that pre-1960 vintage cards would be my primary focus (an interesting move, given my net value at the time). Being a longtime, diehard Cleveland baseball fan, my emphasis was almost entirely on the Indians.

After acquiring my first two 1952 Bowman Indians baseball cards, those of longtime catcher Jim Hegan and color barrier breaker Larry Doby, I decided I would stop at nothing until I had the entire team set (which is to say all of the 1952 Bowman Indians). One-by-one, I began acquiring the appropriate cards. Rather proudly, I found myself hyper, or at the very least peripherally, aware of each player in the set and their place in Cleveland Indians lore (even Lou Brissie). Except one. And it was certainly not a name easily forgotten: Luke Easter. A name even more distinctive when you consider his actual first name was 'Luscious'.

A cursory search provided a few intriguing write-ups, but also something of a veil of mystery surrounding the man. What had been written was captivating; a ballplayer, whose age or origin story was never truly known by many of his teammates and associates, literally traveling the world hitting the longest, and most, home runs anyone had ever seen at the time.

A photograph search seared a spectacular image in my mind: four Cleveland Indians, Al Rosen (1953 American League MVP), Joe Gordon (2009 Hall of Fame inductee), Bobby Avila (1954 American League batting champion), and the African American Easter all standing side-by-side. Now, baseball is a game that even now is played professionally by a good number of average-sized men. In 1950, many of the players may have even been considered diminutive. Not Easter. Standing nearly a head taller than all the men, with thick, brawny forearms and biceps, he showed what a six foot, four inch, 240-pound frame looked like, circa 1950.

But the question remained... just who was this fellow?

Luke Easter's life and baseball career can almost be mistaken as a work of fiction. To that point, it has been alleged that the character of Roy Hobbs in Bernard Malamud's 1952 classic novel *The Natural* could have just as easily been a partial composite of Easter. Truly, in no way is this allegation a stretch.

Until Easter was almost 31 years of age, baseball was not his primary source of income. Shut out of Major League Baseball due to the longstanding observation of the racial color barrier, Easter was a day laborer, working a multitude of jobs, while moonlighting as a baseball player. For much of what could be considered his playing career, baseball was merely his trusty side job. What should have been his prime, physical baseball years occurred exactly during those of the Second World War, and Easter played nary a game during those four years.

Knowing this, how is it even possible that upon breaking into Major League Baseball in 1949, taking his first swings at 34 years of age, he would average almost 30 home runs and over 100 runs batted in over his first three full seasons? Easter, the eleventh player to break baseball's color barrier, was destined to face racial scorn at nearly every turn. He responded the only way he knew: hit the ball farther.

Is it possible Luke Easter was slightly more than just a man?

The ball would blister off his bat. It is said that pitchers would routinely duck from his batted balls, thinking they were screaming line drive singles back up the middle – only to turn around and see that the ball had landed in the stands for a home run. He'd often flash a quick smile at the incredulous pitcher while rounding the bases after hitting one of these patented drives, almost as if he'd fooled them with a magic trick.

To back his baseball prowess, Easter had an infectious smile and was unwaveringly kind to nearly everyone he met. He had a tremendously giving heart. He never really gained financial stability until after he had signed his fourth professional contract (when his wife Vergil began taking care of the finances); though he liked to make a flashy purchase here and there, he would ultimately give most of his money away to anyone who asked or who he thought was in need.

He may have remembered your name, he may not have (probably not though, remembering names was not a strong suit for Easter). Either way, he was probably going to address you generically as 'Bub', while simultaneously making you feel like the most important person in the room. It is said that the great Babe Ruth had similar tendencies.

He was one who was never too busy to stop for an autograph; especially for children, who adored him. He had kids of his own, and always had a soft spot for them. Easter was once suspended from one of his minor league teams after having thrown too many baseballs to kids in the stands. After being warned to stop, he would double down, opening up the ballpark fence to allow kids to run on the field after the games had concluded. There were many, and not just children, who were convinced all Easter was missing was a cape.

The trajectory, the timing, the circumstance, the romanticism, the profound local impact of Easter's life and baseball career make his story read like a mythological character.

But Easter was no myth. He was, simply and aptly, sensational.

By my count, Easter hit 650 professional home runs. It is of note that every one of those were clubbed during and after the same season he turned 31 years old. If you were to include home runs he hit while playing semipro ball, or through his extensive barnstorming career, it is possible Easter hit more home runs than anyone who ever lived. He is certainly a player who should garner consideration for the Baseball Hall of Fame in Cooperstown, New York. He has never appeared on a ballot of any kind.

As a racial trailblazer in baseball, he is largely forgotten too, shouldering much of the same racial scorn commonly attributed to Jackie Robinson and other more popular color barrier breakers. Though they shared almost nothing in common, Easter once reassured fellow black teammate Larry Doby, whom Easter noticed didn't take racial barbs in-stride as well as himself, at least visibly, "Look, Larry, you just fight half the world. You leave the other half to me."

To this point, Scott Simkus, a brilliant researcher, writer, and sage on baseball played 'outside the fringe' of the major leagues, accurately stated the historiographical issues with players like Easter and many of his contemporaries:

> "Half of his career, what literally should have been his best years as an athlete, simply doesn't exist...Men like Luke Easter... became poster boys for baseball's Lost Generation. This was the class of ballplayer for whom integration was just five or ten years too late.
>
> Those who preceded the Lost Boys (greats like Satchel Paige and Josh Gibson) had their legends cemented during the golden age of Negro league coverage. Those who followed the Lost Generation (Hank Aaron, Willie Mays, and Ernie Banks) were given the opportunity to prove themselves on the game's biggest stage.
>
> Guys like Easter...get folded into a different category altogether. There were men like Easter

who had partial (albeit late) opportunities in the big leagues..."

I believe the legitimacy of this passage encapsulates my purpose in sharing Easter's thrilling baseball life, and has validated my efforts behind "Folk Hero Forever". I sincerely hope you enjoy the read as much as I have enjoyed discovering and compiling pieces of Luke's life.

I would like to give a heartfelt thank you to the following people for their help, both directly and indirectly, with *Folk Hero Forever:*

A very special thank you to my wife Alicia for all her support, and to our children Greyson, Eleanor, and Harper. All four allowed myself many hours in our already-hectic lives to research and write, frequently well into the early morning hours.

To all the members Painter Family Tribe Roundtable, our yearly spring family gathering and opportunity to talk everything Indians baseball for the better part of six enchanting hours. To the rest of the immediate family as well, Cleveland sports fans all.

Thank you to the Earlham College (Richmond, Indiana) Library, for the many resources provided from your shelves.

Thank you to Jeremy Feador, Cleveland Indians team historian and archivist, who graciously provided many of the images used in this book.

Thank you to the many incredibly passionate writers, followers, and preservationists of Negro League baseball history including Dr. Layton Revel and The Center for Negro League Baseball Research, Peggy Beck, Leslie Heaphy, Lawrence Hogan, Neil Lanctot, Steve Jacobson, Rick Swaine, and the late Jules Tygiel. All of whom had works that greatly aided this pursuit.

Thank you to the aforementioned Scott Simkus, who has succeeded in writing perhaps the most compelling book about baseball that I have ever read.

To the 'statheads' over at BaseballReference.com. This endeavor would have been nearly impossible without the statistical content you all provide, free of charge.

A special thank you to Daniel J. Cattau, Justin Murphy, and Joe Posnanski, all of whom have written compelling pieces about Luke in the past.

To the newspaper writers, in particular the late Jim Schlemmer of the *Akron Beacon Journal,* and Hal Lebovitz of the *Cleveland Plain Dealer,* who always covered Luke fairly during his playing days.

To the great Hall of Famer owner Bill Veeck, one of the most, if not the most, progressive figures in Major League Baseball history.

Finally, thank you, the reader. Next time I see you, let's drink a beer and talk about Luke Easter.

# Introduction

## 'A Prodigious Swat'

*'How many home runs could Luke Easter have hit? Shoot. As many as he wanted.'*

-Buck O'Neil, Hall of Fame Negro Leaguer

It was a perfect day for a baseball game. A balmy, high temperature of 90 degrees, aided by scarcely a cloud in the sky. It was June 23, 1950. The place? Cleveland, Ohio. Though the 26,000-plus who went through the turnstiles that day for an afternoon matchup didn't know it, they were about to bear witness to one of the most spectacular moments in the club's 50-year history.

The hometown Cleveland Indians were about 18 months removed from earning the franchise's second World Series title in 1948, having bested the Boston Braves four games to two. 1949 proved to be something of a wash for club; despite retaining most the same roster as the championship season, the team spent nary a day in first place the entire campaign. The third place finish that season marked one of the biggest disappointments in team history at the time.

Indians team owner Bill Veeck had acquired the club in 1946. Veeck, considered something of a showman, was never one to shy away from an opportunity for publicity. Future examples of this include in 1951, while the owner of the St. Louis Browns, he signed the three foot, seven inch Eddie Gaedel to a professional contract (who drew a walk in his only at-bat). In 1979, as owner of the Chicago White Sox, he concocted 'Disco Demolition Night', to which fans could bring their old disco records to the ballpark to be destroyed (it was a disaster).

Towards the end of the disappointing 1949 season, Veeck decided a burial of sorts was in order. The deceased? The American League pennant. On September 23rd, 1949, the day the Indians were mathematically eliminated from the playoffs, a literal pennant was buried, complete with coffin (player/manager Lou Boudreau, the traveling secretary, and other members of the coaching staff served as pall bearers), a band to play the funeral procession, and a simple tombstone ('Here Lies the 1948 Champs'), with a burial site just beyond the outfield wall. Veeck did well, as the gambit brought nearly 30,000 fans through the gates of Cleveland Municipal Stadium. "I thought it was a funny gag," Veeck stated later, "and no one could say it wasn't original…Those who liked it thought it was great; those who didn't thought it was in atrocious taste."[1]

Embroiled in divorce proceedings, the progressive Veeck sold his majority ownership stake in the club to Ellis W. Ryan, a 45-year old local insurance executive to the tune of $2.2 million. The new ownership group immediately installed former Detroit Tigers slugger Hank Greenberg as general manager.[2]

Despite fresh leadership at some of the highest posts, the Opening Day lineup heading into 1950 proved to look very much similar to that of the year before. A noteworthy exception included the globe-trotting, home run-hitting sensation, Luscious 'Luke' Easter would take to right field for the Indians (though he would eventually lay claim to his natural position, first base). Easter, an African American, debuted on August 11, 1949 after an incredible summer with the minor league San Diego Padres, becoming the eleventh player to break the Major League Baseball color barrier.

He would receive scattered at-bats, 54 to be exact, over the final 48 days of the 1949 season. Though he hit just .222 for the season, he did end strongly, with a .343 mark over the final six games.[3] When he broke through with the Indians, Easter could barely walk, still recovering from a knee surgery performed mere weeks before. His offensive presence, on display all season long in

San Diego, was expected to lift the Indians out of the offensive mire they found themselves in most of the season. When the hobbled slugger couldn't provide said lift, he was booed incessantly by the home crowd. As expected, he was booed on the road as well. Racial slurs were lobbed at every stop. Despite making his debut in less than ideal circumstances, the local press, save a few pundits, were incredibly critical towards Easter in 1949.

Easter had originally signed with the Indians on February 19, 1949. Veeck reportedly paid $5,000 for him (with an additional $5,000 more if he made the big league club) from the Homestead Grays, his Negro League club. The Grays had long been considered one of the preeminent Negro League clubs for most of their 38-year existence. When he was signed, he told Veeck he was 27 years old. A career inconvenienced by bigotry and prejudice, Easter had already played a dozen years in a variety of locales before the game was finally integrated in 1947 by Jackie Robinson of the Brooklyn Dodgers.

Like many other stars of the Negro League at the time, Easter shaved some years off his actual age, six years in his case, to improve his odds of catching on with a big league outfit. The maneuver worked, as the actual 33-year old was inked to join the Indians. "I'll be 22 if they want me to be, as long as I get the chance," he purportedly told his family.[4] In doing so, he set off an age debate that would rage for decades among fans and his contemporaries. Easter was a willing participant in the façade as well, playing it rather coyly, even at the end of his life.

Age notwithstanding, one fact about Easter that could not be effectively fabricated was his size; 'Big Luke' measured six foot, four-and-a-half inches, and tipped the weight scales at 240 pounds. He was easily the largest player in the entire organization.

A second undeniable attribute was his affability. The man had yet to meet a stranger his entire life. Throughout his time in Cleveland, Easter loved to attend parties; but not nearly as much as he loved being the life *of* the party. He was known to walk into a social gathering and coolly announce, "'Big Luke' is here. Everything is going to be alright."[5] Folks would immediately flock to him, and his laugh could be heard over everyone else's all evening long. Easter also loved to play cards; his proficiency at the activity would make him friends (and enemies) over the years.

Though the big lefty could pull the baseball with thunderous power, he could hit the ball to all fields. In fact, one of his most memorable (and talked about) home runs to date was one that found its way in the dead center field bleachers at the Polo Grounds, some 485 feet from home plate, while playing for the Homestead Grays. "He hit it halfway up the stands..." his teammate Bob Thurman described. "The thing about it – it was a line drive."[6]

Which brings us back to our aforementioned sunny, June 23, 1950 day. The Indians entered the day in third place at 33-25, 5.5 games behind the league leading Detroit Tigers. But the Indians had won 11 of their previous 14 games, including taking two of three from the New York Yankees the previous three days. The contest against the Bronx Bombers the day before proved full of highlights; Indians ace Bob Feller pitched a complete game to earn his seventh win of the season, and the Indians clubbed five solo home runs as a team en route to tidy 6-2 victory. Two of the round trippers flew off the bat of Easter (the second of which traveled an estimated 440 feet), his eighth and ninth of the season. Easter was beginning to sizzle, and optimism was growing, particularly as the Indians were readying themselves for a weekend home series against the Washington Senators.[7]

21-year old California native Bob Ross was slated to make his first career start for the Senators that Friday, June 23rd. As he had for his previous 35 games, Easter would bat third and play first base. Future Hall-of-Famer Bob Lemon got the ball to start for the Indians.

By the bottom of the sixth inning, the Indians held a 6-1 advantage. They had chased the rookie Ross in the fourth, and 32-year old, one-time All-Star Joe Haynes had come in for a long relief opportunity. Easter continued to ride his hot streak; after grounding out in the first, he planted a three-run homer in the third (his tenth on the season third in two days), and a sacrifice fly in the fourth. Sitting with four runs batted in on the day already, Easter came up to bat for the fourth time on the afternoon in the sixth inning.[8]

With two outs and outfielder Dale Mitchell standing on second, Haynes attempted to pitch around Easter, knowing there was an empty base at first. With Easter exhibiting a good batting eye, the stratagem proved ineffective, and Haynes found himself behind in the count 3-0.

Perhaps it was the months of boos and taunts he had endured in his big league career to this point. Maybe it was the pressure to reinvigorate a club finding itself sagging in the standings less than two years after reaching the game's highest point. Conceivably, it could have his depiction from the press, consistent with the era, as imbecilic or slow-witted. Perhaps all, perhaps none.

Cleveland Municipal Stadium, where the Indians played from 1932 through 1993. It is pictured here in 1954. (Public Domain)

As Easter waited for Haynes' next offering, he stood in his upright stance, virtually motionless in the batter's box, as was his style. The righty released a fastball, right down the center of the plate, undoubtedly an attempt to groove an easy strike in and reclaim the at-bat. Easter was waiting for it, taking a cut at that 3-0 pitch, *CRACK!* With the swing, he unleashed his legendary, colossal power with the ball carrying deep into the right field upper deck of Cleveland Municipal Stadium. The titanic blast had landed over the auxiliary scoreboard, in Section 4 to be exact, a feat that had never been accomplished before in the entire history of the ballpark. In a career that full of home runs that no one seemed to be counting yet everyone spoke of, he had just clubbed his most majestic to date.[9] As Easter rounded the bases, one sportswriter called the scene "eerie", as the shocked crowd couldn't seem to comprehend the magnitude of the blast.

"Luscious Luke Easter, the giant first baseman with a dynamite in his bat, has arrived." The *News-Journal* of Mansfield, Ohio exclaimed the following day.[10]

"There have been a lot of games played in the big stadium since 1931," Legendary editor of *The Akron Beacon Journal* Jim Schlemmer wrote the following day, "but this was the first time anybody ever had driven a ball so far into the upper deck in either left or right. Some gallant sluggers who have prior opportunity include such names as Babe Ruth, Lou Gehrig, Jimmy Foxx, Hank Greenberg, Rudy York, Hal Trosky, Earl Averill, Ralph Kiner, Ted Williams, Joe DiMaggio, Tommy Henrich..."[11]

Schlemmer continued "There is no immediate chance to get an accurate measurement on the distance of this prodigious swat. Nor would such knowledge change its value."[12]

The 'prodigious swat' was Easter's fourth in just two days, and his eleventh on the season. Despite battling sometimes crippling pain from surgically-repaired knees, Luke Easter was playing as well as he ever had at the big league level. Engineering students from nearby Case Institute of Technology (Now Case Western Reserve) converged on the scene to get the ball's actual distance traveled. Their conclusion? A whopping 477 feet. It was the longest ball ever hit in Cleveland Municipal Stadium.[13]

Having played organized baseball for over a decade, the extraordinary Easter had arrived indeed.

# 1.

## From the Delta to the Gateway City

*"We'd play ball just about all day long..."*[1]

-J.C. Easter, brother of Luke Easter

Upon examining the back of Easter's 1952 baseball card from the Bowman Gum Company, it lists his birthdate as 'Aug. 4, 1921' and birthplace as 'St. Louis, MO'. This is the data that followed him for essentially his entire playing career.[2] If the Easter family Bible is any indication, his true origins lay in the heart of the Delta, Jonestown, Mississippi, where he was actually born on August 4, 1915. His Christian name was 'Luscious'.[3]

Jonestown, located in Coahoma County, rests about 70 miles southwest of Memphis, and about 350 miles directly south of his fabled birthplace of St. Louis. Jonestown, according to the 1910 census, had a population of 367 people. By 1920, there were 469 residents of the town. The town would barely clear the thousand mark during Easter's lifetime.[4]

Dating back to the 1870's, Coahoma County had been predominantly an African American community. There were two large plantations that surrounded the town, and the cotton industry was still regarded as king, well after the American Civil War. Though slavery was outlawed, its sister institution of sharecropping thrived in many southern states. As was the case throughout most of the country, segregation was legal and sanctioned by way of the Jim Crow laws, which permeated in various (and traditional) ways throughout the town. For instance, whites had their own Baptist church and the blacks had their own.

By way of the Supreme Court case *Plessy v. Ferguson,* it was all but ensured that blacks did not receive the same level of education as their white counterparts did in the area, as the schools were also segregated. Black children could typically only attend class from January to March, on account of being needed to work in the cotton fields. As the young pupils grew to be a bit more able-bodied, it wasn't uncommon they wouldn't go back to school at all, opting to work full-time in the cotton fields.[5]

To further prove the disparity in education, when examining the census numbers contemporary with Easter's birth, the percentage of illiterate whites in the county stood at 1.2%. When considering blacks in Coahoma County, the number leapt to a 34.2% illiteracy rate.[6]

Between 1877 and 1950, Mississippi also had among the highest number of racially-charged lynchings in the country. Among the 77 Mississippi counties that reported instances of lynchings, Coahoma County had the 12th-highest number, with 13 during that span.[7]

Luke Easter was one of seven children born to James and Maude Easter. According to census data, the Easters were married in 1905, when Maude was 20 and James was 23. Unlike many of their fellow community members, the Easters owned their own land, and wouldn't have been described as poverty-stricken. James Easter had attended the Tuskegee Institute, among the famed historically black colleges and universities (HBCU), in Tuskegee, Alabama. Aside from being founded by George Washington Carver, the Institute would go on to earn fame by training and producing some of the finest pilots during the Second World War. He and Maude owned multiple farmland plots in the Jonestown area; they were decidedly members of the working class, and they were, for the most part, able to make ends meet for their family.[8]

The Mississippi Delta would have been much more renowned for music at this time than baseball. Delta blues was one of the earliest forms of the blues musical genre, and was slowly proliferating across the country during the early decades of the 20th century. Champions of the movement included Tommy Johnson, Freddie Spruell, and Robert Patton.

In 1922, tragedy struck the Easters as Maude contracted tuberculosis and passed away. In the early portions of the twentieth century, tuberculosis was among the leading cause of death in America. Little is known about Mrs. Easter. The young Easter was seven years old and had five siblings at the time. "We really didn't know what we had lost," Easter's sister Minnie said years later.[9]

Two years after the death of his wife, James Easter decided there was little left for his family in the Mississippi Delta, opting to join his brother who was already living on the south side of St. Louis.[10]

The Easters, like so many other African Americans living in the Deep South in the 1910's and 1920's, took part in what eventually became known as 'The Great Migration'. During this time, roughly 1.6 million African Americans left the rural South to industrial centers in the North (a 'Second Great Migration' after the Great Depression would lead an additional five million north). They left the South to escape persecution, intending to attempt to outrun the Jim Crow Laws (though it would be found that these could not be simply escaped from), and to seek out more diversified economic opportunities.

It was during this time that the African American populations in New York, Philadelphia, Chicago, Detroit, Pittsburgh, and St. Louis skyrocketed. In the case of Detroit, the African American population multiplied nearly nineteen times over in 30 years. St. Louis, where the Easters settled, there were nearly 100,000 more African Americans living there in 1940 as opposed to 1910.[11] In general, the population grew nearly 13 percent from 1910 to 1920, from about 687,000 to nearly 773,000.[12]

Upon the family's arrival in St. Louis, James Easter took up a job sweeping up sand in a glass factory. He would ultimately remarry, taking the hand of another Mississippi transplant, Annie White in 1924, the year the family arrived in St. Louis.[13]

Whether it was the Mississippi Delta or St. Louis, the Jim Crow Laws persisted. Not long before the Easter's had arrived in the city, there had been a large race riot in St. Louis in 1917, where dozens of blacks had been killed, and hundreds of homes on the east side of the city were burned to the ground. The riot, starting in late May and ending in early July, began with three thousand whites converging on the east side of the city; the result of tensions boiling over regarding 470 African American workers being hired to replace white ones during a labor strike of the Aluminum Ore Company.[14]

Incredibly, even with such a sterling example to prove otherwise, the segregation in St. Louis would still be considered fairly mild when compared to that of the South, as historian Bruce Olson states:

> "Schools in St. Louis were segregated but voting by black men was open. Blacks and whites rode the streetcars together with no front-to-back seating by color, as was the law in the South. A black man in St. Louis was not required to step aside on the sidewalk for a white. Parks and libraries were integrated, but lunch counters were not; nor were races allowed to mix at swimming pools. Entertainment was inconsistent, with whites listening to black ragtime players and blacks attending the World's Fair, generally free to go where they pleased. Theaters were segregated."[15]

As the Easters undoubtedly discovered early on in their tenure in the big city, St. Louis was a baseball town. This would have most certainly differed from the culture in the South. The title of baseball town manifested itself in a multitude of ways; for one, the preeminent baseball publication, *The Sporting News,* was founded by Alfred Spink and based in St. Louis. St. Louis was also the smallest city to accommodate two Major League Baseball teams, with the Cardinals and the Browns (later to become the Baltimore Orioles).

The Cardinals won the 1926 World Series with a team that featured future Hall-of-Famers Jim Bottomley, Rogers Hornsby, Billy Southworth, Chick Hafey, and Pete Alexander. 'Dizzy' Dean and the famed 'Gashouse Gang' would follow the World Series team by less than a decade.[16] Sometimes, when the young Easter came about extra money, he would catch a trolley to Sportsman's Park and watch the Cardinals. Undeterred if he didn't have enough money for an actual ticket to the game, he would sometimes settle for viewing the contests through holes in the stadium fence. At the time, African American spectators were relegated to the right field seating in the 'Colored Only' section for the Cardinals (left field for the Browns). His favorite Cardinal was the slick-fielding first baseman Bottomley.[17]

The Browns, who shared Sportsman's Park with the Cardinals, were generally considered a lowly franchise, ending most seasons towards the bottom of the standings. Even so, the club featured Hall of Famer George Sisler for the better part of the 1920's, and the skilled outfield trio of Ken Williams, Baby Doll Jacobson, and Jack Tobin (who all habitually cleared the .300 batting average mark).[18]

Essentially in-step with their white counterparts, African Americans had also been playing organized baseball since the 1870's. 'Blackball' (also stylized as 'black ball'), as it became known as, was originally used as a pejorative term for African Americans playing the sport, though the expression was later very much embraced by the black community. Though there were blips of national relevancy, blackball had largely been relegated to the fringes of the sporting culture. Blackball teams often "took to the road in early spring, and from then until late fall, they played a ballgame almost every day, meeting black teams and white teams in farm villages and big cities, on sandlots and in major league stadiums."[19]

By the 1920's, the African American brand of baseball began to thrive in the city of St. Louis. Often, the teams didn't just thrive, but showed their mettle, too. In a single October week in 1920, the St. Louis Giants, an all-black outfit formed in 1906 by saloonkeeper, promoter, and blackball pioneer Charley Mills,[20] defeated their white crosstown rivals, the Cardinals, 5-4 in an exhibition game that publicly irritated the Spink family. They then proceeded to defeat the 'Phillies', an all-star team led by Bob Meusel of the Yankees, 7-1.[21]

This wouldn't prove to be an anomalous blip, either. Negro League teams would play well over .500 baseball (128 wins against 115 losses, .527 winning percentage) in exhibition games against Major League clubs during the first half of the 20th century.[22]

St. Louis had her share of blackball heroes; most of whom played for the St. Louis Stars (Mills sold the Giants after the 1921 season, and the club was quickly renamed the 'Stars') including James 'Cool Papa' Bell, Mule Suttles, Oscar Charleston, and Willie Wells (all members of the Baseball Hall of Fame). Wells is widely credited with wearing the first batting helmet during a game in 1942, donning a construction hard hat after taking a beaning to the head earlier against the same pitcher.[23]

James 'Cool Papa' Bell was one of the fastest players to ever play the game. He donned a St. Louis Stars uniform from 1922 through 1931. (Public Domain)

The Stars had joined the upstart Negro National League in 1920, and they played their home games at Stars Park, built in 1922 which seated 10,000 fans.[24] The Stars would go on to capture three Negro National League Pennants, with titles in 1928, 1930, and 1931.[25]

In the midst of what would become known as the greatest recessions in American history, The Great Depression, James Easter was fortunately never out of work long. Luke and some of his siblings split time between the St. Louis public schools and working (Luke held jobs shining shoes, blocking hats, and pressing suits at a dry cleaner). When not occupied with either,

Luke and his younger brother J.C. would play baseball. While baseballs and bats may have been hard to come by, broomsticks and soda-bottle tops were not. It was said that Easter developed his batting eye by taking swings at the caps, which had a propensity of twisting, turning, and fluttering after being tossed.

By the time Easter had reached high school, he had reasoned that the level of education he would obtain would not affect his future employment prospects; therefore, he quit school just before the ninth grade and went to work for a paint company on the south side of St. Louis. Concurrently, the teenage Easter would play both recreational (yet very competitive) sandlot baseball and softball as well.[26]

In an era where the average male stood five feet, seven inches tall, James Easter cut a brawny six foot, one inch, 215 pound frame. It wouldn't have been much of a surprise that some of his children would be a commensurate size. By his late teens, his son Luke stood almost six feet, four inches tall. The young Easter would have most certainly towered over all of his baseball-playing peers. Just as his physical stature grew, so did his acclaim on the sandlot baseball fields. It was clear to many in the St. Louis blackball community that the young, power-hitting Easter was on the come-up.

## 2.

## The Titanium Giants and the Wartime Years

*"Don't look back, someone might be gaining on you."*

*-Satchel Paige, pitching legend, seventh player to break baseball's color barrier*

Through the first three decades of the 20th century, the Negro National League (NLL) represented, by a wide margin, the biggest step of progress in creating organized baseball for African Americans. Founded in 1920, the first eight teams were based primarily in the Midwest; the Indianapolis ABCs, Dayton Marcos, Detroit Stars, Cuban Stars, Kansas City Monarchs, Chicago American Giants, and the Charlie Mills-owned St. Louis Giants. The Chicago club was owned and managed by Andrew 'Rube' Foster, perhaps the most famous blackball pitcher of the time, and certainly among the game's biggest advocates. In 1902, Foster was credited with winning 44 consecutive starts. Pulling most of the strings to get the NLL organized and executed, he proved to be the savviest executive as well.[1]

After the league was formed, it was only natural that Foster selected as president; he soon accumulated roles as secretary-treasurer, chairman of the league's board of directors, and was even tasked with making the schedule.[2] The league flourished financially, particularly the first few seasons.

From a talent standpoint, the NLL was easily sustained. Though a previous attempt at creating a black league had been tried once before (The National Colored Base Ball League was founded in 1887 and only survived one season), it did show Foster that, 'the short time of its existence served to bring out the fact that colored ball players of ability were numerous."[3]

It was also quickly discovered that black teams could drum up interest in the league by 'barnstorming', or playing friendly exhibition games, particularly in the parts of the country that didn't have organized baseball leagues.

The 'Father of Black Baseball', Rube Foster. Pictured here at the 1924 Negro League World Series. (Public Domain)

Unfortunately, halfway through the 1926 season, Foster was committed to a mental institution in Kankakee, Illinois, suffering from extreme paranoia and delusions. He would spend his final four years in the hospital, before ultimately dying in 1930 at age 51.[4]

The NLL would feel Foster's loss in terms of leadership and vision, and it wasn't long before the foundation Foster had worked so diligently at began to fall apart. Mills had sold the St. Louis Giants to a pair of investors Dick Kemp and Dr. Sam Sheppard before the 1922 season, and the team was renamed the St. Louis Stars. Despite the success the team experienced, as evident by three pennant-winning seasons, there was trouble brewing. The city was eyeing the plot of land where Stars Park sat as a potential space for a municipal playground. Even after winning the league title in 1931, ownership revealed a loss of $14,000 at the box office, an abysmal attendance showing.

Shortly after the season ended, the Stars management sold the park to the city, spelling the end of the team.[5] The St. Louis struggles were indicative of the rest of the league, as the whole NLL operation went defunct after the 1931 season, less than a year after her revered founder's passing.

The Stars were effectively dead and their park was soon leveled to the ground, "permanently destroying (Negro) league baseball in St. Louis" many thought at the time.[6] Soon, other independent blackball outfits were formed in St. Louis, but none to the stature of the Stars. Beginning in the early-to-mid 1930's, the St. Louis Giants began popping up (very) occasionally in the local papers when exhibition games were being promoted. The upstart squad was once again owned and funded by none other than the blackball pioneer Charlie Mills.[7]

In the mid-1930's, the Giants picked up their biggest sponsor, The Titanium Pigment Company, a subsidiary of the National Lead Company. Perhaps as something of an homage to the Mills blackball clubs of the past, the team, while effectively integrating their new sponsor in their name, was appropriately dubbed the 'St. Louis Titanium Giants'. Mills would sign many of the former Giants (and Stars) players, though it wouldn't appear as any of the future Hall of Famers laced up for the Titanium Giants.

The semipro outfit, however, would sign (at least) one young up-and-comer. A tall, sinewy, product of the south side of St. Louis, Luke Easter, was inked to the squad in 1935.[8,9] Easter would play mostly right field and first base. Players for the Titanium Giants worked at the Titanium Pigment Company plant during the course of the week, would practice in the evenings, and would barnstorm mostly on the weekends. Players earned $20 a week at the plant, with an additional $10 to $20 coming in from the weekend games. Easter, still filling out his six foot, four inch frame, was a member of the plant's rigging crew, and he built his muscles hauling the heavy machinery. Like many of their contemporaries, there wasn't much press dedicated to a semi-pro barnstorming team who competed outside of league play, short of a box score in the *St. Louis Argus* (a black newspaper), or if Mills took out an advertisement to promote a high-profile upcoming contest.[10]

The Titanium Giants were opportunists, playing whoever would oppose them. The 'season' would generally consist of about a 60 games, and the Titanium Giants annual loss total would hover around six games – this included playing a healthy slate against better-funded Negro League teams as well. They could most certainly score runs; in one ten-game stretch in 1938, the Giants banged out 113 hits and scored 102 runs. In 1940, they defeated all six of the Negro American League teams they played, including the famed Kansas City Monarchs 3-2. The owner of the Monarchs, J.L. Wilkinson (one of the few Caucasian owners in the Negro Leagues), expressed interest in signing the entire Titanium Giants squad after the contest. Though more than likely just a gesture of respect, it certainly spoke to the acclaim of the barnstorming club.[11]

Easter's raw power at the plate was felt early on by his teammates. In fact, the semipro factory team would often sit on the bench before and after games and argue which of Easter's home runs had traversed the furthest distance.[12]

In 1939, Easter was selected to play in the *St. Louis Argus* East-West All-Star game as a representative of the Giants.[13]

Even early in his playing days, Easter gained the reputation as having a gregarious personality. When speaking of his former teammate, Giants shortstop Jesse Askew said that Easter was a 'big, playful fellow...he had all the natural ability.'

Aside from playing, it wasn't uncommon that Easter would often drive to watch tournaments on the weekends if the Titanium Giants weren't scheduled to play. He would sometimes volunteer as a 'ringer' if one of the teams needed an extra player. He would often be joined by teammates, notably Sam 'The Jet' Jethroe, a fellow Giant outfielder. Jethroe, allegedly so quick he could "outrun the word of God",[14] was perhaps the fastest player of his time, short of 'Cool Papa' Bell. Jethroe had a similar trajectory as Easter; though a couple years younger, he would certainly employ his 'baseball age' as well, effectively shaving a couple years off to make himself more desirable to Major League Baseball teams. He was also born in Lowndes County Mississippi, about 175 miles southeast of Jonestown. Like Easter's, Jethroe's family also moved north in the 1920's, settling in East St. Louis, Illinois.

Easter, Jethroe, and another other teammate made an early spring trip to Memphis, Tennessee to watch (or play in, sources differ) a weekend tournament in 1941. On the return trip to St. Louis, Jethroe fell asleep behind the wheel and the car was involved in an accident. Though it would appear that Jethroe and the other passenger were relatively unharmed, Easter suffered a broken ankle, a banged-up knee, and other injuries, causing him to miss several weeks of the 1941 season (though he would return by season's end). The injuries he suffered in the accident would prove to be a source of physical pain throughout his playing career.[15]

It can be considered all but certain that had Easter been born white, he would have undoubtedly been playing at least low-level, affiliated minor league baseball by 1940. Professional scouts routinely scoured hundreds of amateur and semi-pro leagues across the country for their parent clubs, signing up new, young, talented players on the spot. Unfortunately for Easter, and many others, there was nowhere near that level of sophistication among black professional leagues.

December 7, 1941 proved to be the day that would spell the beginning of end of the Titanium Giants, as the United States was 'suddenly and deliberately attacked by naval and air forces of the Empire of Japan.' A date, President Roosevelt prognosticated 'which will live in infamy.' All told, nearly 2,400 American soldiers, sailors, and civilians were killed during a surprise attack of an American naval base at Pearl Harbor, Hawaii.[16]

The country charged into what would become known as the Second World War. For the United States, it proved to be a four-year struggle with the Axis Powers, consisting of Japan, Germany, and Italy.

In-step with the rest of the country, baseball also mobilized for war. Bob Feller, the ace of the Cleveland Indians who had already accumulated 107 wins by age 22, famously enlisted in the Navy two days after Pearl Harbor.[17] In the spring of 1945, the *New York Times* published an article and corresponding statistics that there were about 5,800 professional baseball players active at the time of the Pearl Harbor attack, and that nearly 5,400 had gone into the military to support the war effort, equivalent to 93%. Every level of every baseball league, both white and black were affected by the conflict.[18]

Luke Easter himself would be drafted into the war effort as well. According to his draft card, he was inducted into the Army on June 22, 1942. His employer was still listed as the 'The Titanium Pigment Company'. Interestingly, his card read his age to be '25 years old'. By the time he was drafted and entered the service, Easter would have been 27 years old. It is possible he filled out his draft card early in 1941 (as many did) before his 26th birthday, but it is certainly possible that Easter was being a bit agile with his age. His father, James Easter was listed as his emergency contact. It is revealed that the father and son only lived 1.2 miles away from each other based on the addresses offered on the draft card. At the bottom was the signature of 'Luscious Easter'.

Easter was sent to basic training at Fort Leonard Wood, Missouri, located in the Ozark Mountains about 150 miles from St. Louis. The base, originally opened in 1940 to support the pending war efforts, and is still presently active.

As a result of the physical demands of basic training, Easter found the daily pain in his ankle to be excruciating. After several months of gritting through the discomfort, he was prompted to see the Army medical staff at the base. It was discovered that Luke's injuries from the car accident had not properly healed, or were not given sufficient time to heal before returning back to work and baseball. A little over a year after reporting to Fort Leonard Wood, he was honorably discharged from the Army on July 3, 1942. He would finish out the war working at a shipyard in Portland, Oregon continuing to support the war effort.[19]

With most of the sport's stars serving the country abroad and at home, baseball spent a few years more or less out of the public's collective conscience. While play for Major League Baseball continued during the war, few thought of it as anything more than just a placeholder while the conflict was raging. Frank Graham, a famed New York sportswriter, likened the starless, replacement player-laden brand of ball to "the tall men against the fat men at the company picnic."[20] A bit dramatic, perhaps, but the sentiment was felt by many fans as stars such as Feller, Ted Williams, Joe DiMaggio, and Stan Musial supported the war effort. Baseball fans at home would often see players who were either too old or too young to be drafted, such as 15-year old Joe Nuxhall, who suited up for the Reds in 1944.

Purportedly, during the wartime years of 1941 through most of 1945, Luke Easter did not play a single inning of baseball.

Traditionally, a baseball hitter's peak is commonly attributed to the age 27-30 seasons. Easter found himself to be not just an unfortunate victim of circumstance (segregated baseball), but also timing; his somewhat forced hiatus from baseball (supporting the war efforts at home) occurred from the time he was 27 to 30 years old.

To this point in his life, Luke had only played semi-pro, part-time baseball. Playing baseball full-time was not an option. For blacks, baseball was generally played in conjunction with a steady-paying job. In fact, at the time, it was not uncommon for black ball players to turn down opportunities to play elsewhere for more money if there was not a steady, 9-to-5 job attached to the offer. While in St. Louis, Easter himself balked at several baseball offers, not wanting to leave his well-paying job as an evening security guard, which supplemented his earnings from baseball and titanium plant.[21]

While unfortunate, this was the reality for dozens (if not hundreds) of elite baseball players if they happened to be black.

As the war wound down, Easter moved to Chicago, Illinois. He ultimately found work the summer of 1945 in a war chemical plant.[22] He would often hang around the ball field at Washington Park, a nearly all-black neighborhood with a municipal park of the same name, hoping to catch on with one of the all-black teams. The 30-year old Easter would loiter around the backstop, hollering at the players and coaches to give him a turn at the plate. When finally given an at-bat one day, Easter socked a long home run. Immediately after the at-bat, a spectator offered Easter $18 a week to play on his traveling team.[23] Despite the lull in his playing career, he still boasted his past power, and the crowds still marveled at the home run hitting ability of the newcomer Luke Easter.

World War II would see its formal end on September 2, 1945. Simultaneously, Luke Easter found himself back in the game.

As he had before the war, Easter played recreational softball in addition to baseball. While playing in a tournament in St. Louis in the spring of 1946, he belted two long, tape measure home runs, 'Easter Eggs' as they would become famously known. Unbeknownst to Easter, the interest of a spectator in the crowd that day was certainly piqued.

# 3.

## Abe Saperstein and the Crescents

*"They used to say 'if they found a good black player, they'd sign him'. They was lying."*

-Cool Papa Bell, regarding the pre-1947 baseball color barrier

As told in a later feature story about Easter in *Collier's*, the tale of his discovery sounds almost apocryphal. Though it very well may have been, it still seems fitting for Luke Easter.

Quincy Smith was a 28-year old outfielder for the Cincinnati Crescents, who would have been considered the equivalent of a triple-A Negro League team.[1] Smith, a veteran of both the Cleveland Buckeyes and the Birmingham Black Barons[2], just happened to be watching from the stands when Easter hit his two long home runs in St. Louis. He was taken aback by Easter. Smith, who had been playing professionally for years, was probably convinced he knew of everyone on the black circuit, yet he had never heard of or seen the giant lefty. When he was back in Chicago, he stopped by the office of Abe Saperstein, owner of the Crescents. In addition to the Crescents, the 44-year old Saperstein also famously owned the barnstorming basketball outfit, the Harlem Globetrotters.

"We need a couple of additional hitters for the club this summer," Saperstein told Smith. "Do you know of any prospects?"

"I saw this big guy hit a softball about nine miles in St. Louis the other day," Smith replied. "Fellow by the name of Easter."[3]

Whether or not the encounter actually happened as reported in *Collier's* remains to be seen. Smith may have been a baseball voice that Saperstein trusted; at one point, Saperstein also owned the Black Barons, a team Smith was also a veteran of. Regardless, the desperation for players that Saperstein was feeling was great enough to merit Easter an invitation to the Crescents spring training camp in 1946 down in New Orleans, Louisiana.

Saperstein, despite being a white man himself, would prove to be a titan of the African American sporting life in the 20$^{th}$ century. He was born in London, England of Polish Jews in 1902, and immigrated to America at the age of five. He matured to be a short man, only five foot, three inches tall, deemed too small to have ever garnered much consideration himself as a basketball or baseball player. As Ben Green, a Harlem Globetrotters historian stated, Saperstein "overcame his physical limitations with boundless drive and ambition, a ferocious work ethic, uncanny relationship skills, and an all-encompassing marketing vision constrained only by the boundaries of space and time...He is a complicated, multilayered personality – a pioneering humanist to some (the Abe Lincoln of Basketball) and a racist huckster to others, the purveyor of a demeaning minstrel show for whites."[4]

As complex of a character Saperstein proved to be, whether through savvy or desperation, he served as the outlet that provided Luke Easter an opportunity to play baseball professionally, and full-time, for the first time in his life. He was 31 years old.

Easter joined the team in New Orleans for spring training that year. His power immediately impressed. He had a good enough spring where we was awarded the starting first base position for the Crescents, and would be paid $325 a month.[5] This nearly doubled his pay from what he was making working at the Titanium Pigment Company and playing for the Titanium Giants.

The Crescents, though based out of Cincinnati, really didn't have a home field to speak of. They would often play at Crosley Field, the home of the Cincinnati Reds. When the famed, all-white, barnstorming squad the House of David came to Cincinnati on May 31, 1946, it was the Crescents battled them at Crosley Field. It was the first time in the House of David's storied, nearly three decade history they had played in the Queen City.[6] The Crescents belonged to no league, but would play anyone and everyone with whom they could obtain booking. According to *Collier's*, "the team played practically every night, making long jumps in an old bus which the players took turns driving. Easter served with the rest as a 'bussie' (the traditional baseball nickname for bus drivers) and paced the team's attack with his big bat." [7]

*Abe Saperstein, famed owner of the Cincinnati Crescents and Harlem Globetrotters. (Public Domain)*

As early as July 23rd, Easter had hit his 41st round tripper of the 1946 campaign. "Easter Whole Show as Crescents Win" the *Cincinnati Enquirer* proclaimed after the Crescents 11-2 win over the Memphis Red Sox at Crosley Field, the *Enquirer* proceeded to dub him "Negro baseball's leading home run hitter" in the game's summary.[8]

Nearly a week later, the *Enquirer* was still chattering about Easter's big fly from July 23rd, stating that "Big Luscious (Luke) Easter, Crescent first-baseman, still has fans talking as the result of his 41st homer which he unfurled into the bleacher entrance against the Red Sox. The blow was one of the longest homers ever hit here and since then Easter has lined out two more".[9] According the paper, he had 43 home runs, as was "rapidly becoming one of the biggest stars in baseball."[10]

Similar to when Easter played for the Titanium Giants, the Crescents also had a penchant for beating teams that should have ostensibly been much more talented than they. "Crescents are Jinx to League Clubs", the *Enquirer* boasted in mid-August. "The Cincinnati Crescents will be out for their fifth and sixth victories over Negro American League opposition when they play the Chicago American Giants in a double-header at Crosley Field Sunday." According to the report, there was also to be a pregame hitting contest between the teams with Easter headlining for the Crescents and Eddie 'Pepper' Young (a seven-year veteran) for the American Giants.[11]

Perhaps one of the most acclaimed tournaments of the day was the annual, late summer *Denver Post* Tournament. Sponsored by the newspaper and taking place in Colorado, the event was declared the 'World Series of semi-pro baseball'. Started in 1915, it was an all-white series until Negro League teams began to merit invites in 1934. Only ten teams were invited yearly; participants would range from Negro League teams (the established Kansas City Monarchs), all-white barnstorming teams (the aforementioned House of David), all-black barnstorming teams (the upstart Cincinnati Crescents), as well as Hispanic and other racially mixed squads. It was America's first truly integrated baseball event, and even had a grand prize of up to $7,500.[12]

The Crescents were invited to play in the tournament in 1946. Aside from Easter, Cool Papa Bell also starred on the team. Satchel Paige (who gained much of his earlier fame as a result of his heroics in the 1934 *Denver Post* Tournament, the first year blacks could participate) would lace up for the Crescents that year as well as something of a ringer for the club. They would actually make the finals that year (and in 1947 as well).[13] In 1946, the Crescents would drop the championship bout to Syd Pollack's Ethiopian Clowns squad (later to move to Indianapolis while keeping the Clowns moniker). The Clowns had previously won the tournament in 1941 as well.[14]

That fall, Saperstein took the Crescents to Honolulu, Hawaii, arriving from San Francisco on September 20.[15] The Crescents were slated to play in 19 games during their stay in Hawaii's fall league. During the circuit, Easter smacked 12 home runs, leading all hitters. The games were played at Honolulu Park on the island, where many big leaguers played ball while in the service during World War II. Local observers noted that Easter's home runs well-exceeded the distance of those hit by baseball's most legendary power hitters of the day, including the home runs slugged by 'The Yankee Clipper', Joe DiMaggio, who had played at the field while a member of the United States Air Force.[16]

About a week into the trip, a trio of sport stars paid the schoolyard kids at Kumaiki Middle School an impromptu visit, undoubtedly organized by Saperstein. Included in the threesome was Easter, Reese 'Goose' Tatum of both baseball and Harlem Globetrotters fame, and the world-famous Olympic sprinter Jesse Owens (recipient of four gold medals at the 1936 games in Berlin, Germany). Each athlete gave the youths a motivational speech, then were "besieged with autograph fans... Youngsters packed around the stars with notebooks and paper, jamming up the schedule which had originally been planned to include a few baseball and basketball exhibition plays."[17]

While his hitting remained phenomenal as a member of the Crescents, Easter was able to hone in on the defensive portion of his game at first base. This was thanks to the coaching received by the most seasoned manager he had played under, Winfield Welch. Welch, another forgotten blackball pioneer, cut his teeth in the 1920's as a member of the New Orleans Black Pelicans. He would go on to manage the Shreveport Acme Giants and the Birmingham Black Barons.[18] A jack-of-all-trades, Welch was also the chief bellman at the largest Shreveport hotel, and also served Saperstein as the head coach of the Harlem Globetrotters for a time.[19]

Not surprisingly, it wouldn't appear as though records were fully kept for the Crescents, therefore it is not known exactly how many home runs Easter ultimately hit in that 1946 season, outside of the (at least) 55 reported. There have also been multiple claims, that

Easter hit 74 home runs. The *Sporting News* reported that Easter had hit .415 and drove in 152 runs that season.[20] It can be safely assumed that dozens of contests were played without statistics kept or reported.

A few years later, Easter was asked by *Collier's* what he remembered about his tenure with the Crescents and his 1946 campaign. Despite not keeping spot-on statistical records, Easter said he remembered that he 'hit a lotta homers'.[21] He would also say multiple times over the years, "I hit em, then forget 'em," when talking about his home runs.[22]

Easter's spectacular 1946 season was the beginning to what would be Easter's first taste of what would become a bit of national exposure. Easter had thrived on the biggest stage he had played on up to that point. 1947 would prove to be the most important season in baseball history, with Easter continuing his improbable rise.

# 4.

# 1947: The Color Barrier Falls, an Heir Apparent Rises

*Remember I told you about the catcher pounding his mitt when Satchel Paige was throwing the ball? That catcher's name was Josh Gibson. Josh Gibson could hit the ball! Let me tell you, he could hit the ball! He could hit that ball! He could hit that ball so hard people called him the Black Babe Ruth. But people who really knew their baseball called Babe Ruth the white Josh Gibson!*[1]

*-Lorne Brown, excerpt from 'Tales from the Negro Leagues'*

It would not appear as though Luke Easter and Josh Gibson were associates. They were never teammates, and it's not believed they ever they played against each other.[2] Serendipitously, yet tragically, their careers will be forever linked.

Josh Gibson was born in rural Buena Vista, Georgia on December 21, 1911. Like many African American families of the time, the Gibson family moved north to Pittsburgh when Gibson was 12 years old. Similar to Easter, Gibson grew quickly to be a brawny young man in high school, maturing to his adult size of six foot, one inch, 200-plus pounds while still in high school.[3]

Gibson soon began playing baseball, and he quickly established a reputation while still a teenager of having massive power behind his colossal swing. In 1930, then just 18 years old, Gibson was signed by Cumberland 'Cum' Posey's Homestead Grays, who were based in Pittsburgh.

Gibson would spend much of the next 15 years in a Grays uniform, racking up legendary home runs along the way. In 1938, Gibson hit perhaps one of the most famous home run of his career, a mammoth drive to right field that allegedly left Yankee

Stadium while his Homestead Grays were battling the New York Lincoln Giants in postseason play. The ball allegedly traveled 505 feet, but had been reported by *Sporting News* to have traveled as far as 580 feet.[45]

Washington Senators owner Clark Griffith once claimed that Josh Gibson hit more home runs to the distant left field bleachers in the Senators Griffith Field than the entire American League combined.[6]

Like nearly all the stars of the day, black or white, Gibson would barnstorm quite frequently in the offseason, often pairing with Satchel Paige. Paige, a master showman and promoter himself, would make posters for their barnstorming contests that would read: "World's Greatest Home Run Hitter Josh Gibson. Guaranteed to Hit Three Home Runs or Your Money Back". A bold prediction on Paige's part, but "I bet we never gave one penny of that money back," Paige rather proudly proclaimed later.[7]

Gibson would spend nearly his entire career with the Homestead Grays. Though originally based in the Pittsburgh area, were playing most of their home games in the nation's capital by 1943. Between 1930 and 1946, Gibson would hit hundreds of home runs, and the Grays became one of the most popular, if not the most popular, Negro League teams in America. Gibson, joined by teammates Cool Papa Bell, Willie Wells, Oscar Charleston, and Buck Leonard would win the league championship a whopping ten times.[8] Gibson was among the first players to attempt to play baseball year-round. He wound up playing extensively in the Deep South and California, Mexico, Cuba, Puerto Rico, and the Dominican Republic winter leagues as well.

However, by the mid-1940's, Gibson's health was beginning to fail him. He began to drink heavily. The friendly, baby-faced Gibson was a man that his associates noticed had begun spinning out of control. Whatever inner demons he had pent up for his first few decades of life were released, exacerbated by alcohol and possible drug abuse. Less frequently was the jolly, gregarious version of Gibson seen. On New Year's Day in 1943, after intense scrutiny and discipline from the Grays, Gibson was placed under the care of a Pittsburgh mental institution.[9] He had also been suffering from seizures as a result of a brain tumor, which he fell into a coma as a result of. Doctors wanted to operate on the tumor, thinking a procedure would alleviate some cranial pressure off his brain, and would help with his onset of erratic behavior. Gibson, fearing he would become a "vegetable" as the result of any procedure, refused to allow it.[10]

Later that same year, Gibson and Leonard were invited to the office of Clark Griffith, owner of the Washington Senators. Griffith asked the duo if they thought they were capable of playing baseball at the big league level. They affirmed they believed they could. Griffith then warned the two, prophetically, that "If we get you boys, we're going to get the best ones. It's going to break up your league." To which Leonard replied, "Well, if it's going to be better for the players, then it's all right by me." Griffith never came calling after the initial meeting.[11]

*Legendary Negro League slugger Josh Gibson, donning a Homestead Grays uniform in a photograph circa 1931. (Public Domain)*

Miraculously, Gibson returned and continued to play well for the Grays despite his obvious personal and health issues. He routinely pushed his batting average near .400 and continued swatting his patented long ball.

In all, according to the *Negro League Encyclopedia* credited Gibson with hitting 962 home runs in his career, including 84 during the 1936 season.[12] Similar to Luke Easter, there is no way possible to corroborate the home run totals of Josh Gibson.

On the morning of January 20, 1947, Josh Gibson stumbled home to his mother's home after a night of drinking at a couple Pittsburgh watering holes. He looked sick; his weight had dropped to 180 pounds. His sister later said that he had come home, went to bed laughing, and quickly fell asleep. Gibson, a titan of Negro League who perhaps hit more home runs than anyone who ever lived, never made another sound; he was killed by a stroke after going to sleep that morning. He was only 35 years old.[13]

Echoing a lifetime of sentiment, the *Pittsburgh Post-Gazette* called Gibson "the Babe Ruth of negro baseball".[14]

Fifteen months before Gibson's death, the Brooklyn Dodgers announced that they had signed 26-year old Jackie Robinson to a contract. Making the pronouncement on October 23, 1945, Robinson was now positioned to break Major League Baseball's color barrier – the unwritten rule that had barred blacks from competing in the league since its inception.[15]

Robinson was chosen for several reasons. First, he was an outstanding athlete, playing on the baseball, football, basketball, and track team at UCLA. He was the university's first four-sport letter winner. It is of note that the athletic teams at UCLA were already integrated, so he already had a bevy of experience playing with white teammates. Second, he had been commissioned a second lieutenant while serving in the army, showing "that he could deal with prejudice and bigotry in a professional manner" in an integrated Army. Finally, and perhaps most importantly, his "character was his biggest asset. He had the mental discipline and fortitude to 'take' whatever he was confronted with, deal with it and persevere."[16]

The road to Robinson's signing was platted by decades of black pioneers, including Gibson. As far as wider acceptance by what would be considered the "white media" of the day, Paige should garner much of the thanks. Ric Roberts, a writer for the *Pittsburgh Courier* who covered most of Paige's career, penned the following in 1940:

> "For the first time a white magazine had burned incense at the foot of a black man outside the prize ring. Satchel brought people back to the ball game. He got blacks in the habit of going to ball games spending their money, and it caught the eyes of Branch Rickey...Satchel Paige led us to the promised land. He was the guy that gave black baseball its first real economic solvency."[17]

For long after his death, there was a myth that Gibson had died of a broken heart, suffered from not being chosen to break baseball's long-observed color line. Though false, the myth was promulgated by his former teammates and associates. In reality, Josh Gibson was just another victim of his era.

The reaction to Robinson's signing was varied. Paige told the *New York Times* that "They didn't make a mistake in signing Robinson. They couldn't have picked a better man." While Rogers Hornsby, former St. Louis Cardinal and future Hall of Famer stated that "A mixed baseball team differs from other sports because ball players on the road live much closer together. It won't work."[18]

Heading into the 1947 campaign, the Grays brass had some tough decisions to make. Owner, founder, and one-time player Cumberland 'Cum' Posey had died a year earlier in March of 1946 of cancer. The club had missed the Negro League World Series in 1946 for the first time in four years (winning two of their four total appearances to-date). The Newark Eagles, led by Larry Doby and Monte Irvin, defeated Buck O'Neil's Kansas City Monarchs in a tightly-contested seven game series to bring the league championship to New Jersey for the first time ever.[19]

Rufus 'Sonnyman' Jackson, part-owner of the Grays and a confidant to Posey while he was living, presumably took over the day-to-day operations of the club. The power of Gibson was certainly a need to be replaced. Though attendance issues had long plagued black franchises, the struggle at the turnstiles began to seep into Griffith Stadium, where the Grays, one of the oldest franchises in black baseball, played most of their home games. It didn't take long to find a possible solution for both.

By early 1947, Jackson found his man. Luke Easter officially signed a contract to play right field and first base for the Homestead Grays of the Negro National League. He had arisen as the heir apparent to the late Gibson, and he found himself easily on his biggest stage to date. As one historian wrote, "Baseball had finally caught up with Luke Easter."[20] Present while he signed on the contract's dotted line was Jackson and Seward 'See' Posey, older brother of Cum Posey, and business manager for the Grays. The contract paid Easter the handsome sum of $700 ($1,100 has also been reported) a month. The slugger would see most of his time in left field since the legendary (and future Hall of Famer) Buck Leonard was holding down first base.

After a strong spring training in Havana, Cuba, Jackie Robinson got the nod to begin the 1947 campaign with the Brooklyn Dodgers (he had spent the 1946 season with the Montreal Royals, Brooklyn's AAA affiliate). Robinson was penciled into the starting lineup for the April 15 Opening Day contest against the Boston Braves. Though a natural second baseman, Robinson started at first base since the Dodgers already had an established second baseman, Eddie Stanky. 14,000 black spectators went through the turnstiles to see the historic event.[21] The color barrier, omnipresent in organized baseball for 75 years, had finally fallen. The Dodgers would go on to beat the Braves, 5-3. Robinson scored a run and played an error-free brand of first base.[22]

Facing blistering racial scrutiny for most of the entire season, Robinson hardly wavered visibly, just as Rickey had instructed. A blend of congratulatory notes and also death threats filled the team's mailbox. In May, Herb Pennock, the general manager of the Philadelphia Phillies and former big league pitcher, threatened to boycott their scheduled May 9 game against the Dodgers in Philadelphia unless Robinson stayed home in Brooklyn. The Dodgers called their bluff, stating they would accept a forfeited victory if needs be, and the game was played.[23] Robinson doubled, singled, and scored two runs in the extra inning loss.[24]

Back in the nation's capital, Easter had been deemed the successor to Gibson for the Grays. So much so, in fact, management handed Easter the number 20 jersey, Gibson's old number. Many found the move to be distasteful mere months after Gibson's death, but it certainly served as a not-so-subtle reminder of Easter's expectations heading into his first season with the Grays. So did Easter's paycheck, which was among the highest on the team.[25]

A month into Robinson's rookie year in 1947, Cleveland Indians owner Bill Veeck announced that the Indians "engaged the services of Abe Saperstein's organization for the purpose of scouting Negro talent on an international scale". If anyone had the corner on black talent in America, Veeck reasoned, it was Saperstein. The two were also friends. The top recommendation to Veeck was the 23-year old second baseman from the Newark Eagles, Larry Doby. Veeck negotiated a $15,000 purchase price for Doby from the Eagles on July 3, 1947.[26]

Just two days later, on July 5, 1947, Larry Doby entered the Indians game against the Chicago White Sox as a pinch hitter for pitcher Bryan Stephens in the top of the seventh inning[27], thus becoming the first black player in the American League. The crowning achievement was met with much less fanfare than Robinson, but the vitriolic opposition was certainly comparable, prompting Doby to later state that "You didn't hear much about what I was going through because the media didn't want to repeat the same story."[28]

Like Robinson had also experienced, some of the opposition arose from his new teammates.

Upon entering the Indians clubhouse for the first time and introducing himself, four of his new teammates refused to shake his hand. After jogging out to his first practice, no one would take warm-up tosses with him for several minutes. Doby stood alone, dejected, until second baseman Joe Gordon waved his glove at Doby to have him throw him the ball. For the rest of the season, Doby warmed up with Gordon. Doby never forgot Gordon's graciousness that day. Catcher Jim Hegan and Bill McKechnie on the coaching staff were also particularly accommodating to the black youngster. But there were still issues with some on the team. When manager Lou Boudreau asked Doby to take some reps at first base one day during warmups, none of the Indians' first basemen would share their mitts with him.[29]

*23-year old Larry Doby, made his debut for the Indians on July 5, 1947, thus breaking the American League color barrier. He followed Dodger Jackie Robinson by mere weeks. (Public Domain)*

Veeck, who would lend vital organs to win (and simultaneously make the turnstiles click), stated that when Doby was signed, "We received 20,000 letters, most of them in violent and sometimes obscene protest...I wrote [that] I was sure they would agree that any man should be judged on his personal merit and allowed to exploit his talents to fullest, whether he happened to be black, green, or blue with pink dots."[30]

Doby would appear in 28 more games for the Indians that year, mostly in a pinch-hitting capacity.[31]

Easter began his Grays tenure with a splash; "Easter Homers in Debut" exclaimed the *Pittsburgh Courier* on May 3, 1947. "Off to an explosive start, the 6,000 fans saw Luke Easter live up to advance billing when, in the first frame of the opener, he sledged an awesome 435-foot homer high into the left-center stands with Sam Bankhead aboard." Homering in his first Negro League at-bat was just adding another entry into the mythos of the slugger. The Grays would split the exhibition doubleheader against the New York Black Yankees.[32]

Two weeks later, another local rag wrote, "Luscious (Luke) Easter, left fielder for the Homestead Grays, is the most notable addition to Negro baseball this season. A product of St. Louis, Easter, 6 feet 6 inches and weighing 245, is expected to develop into the home run king of the league."[33] Though his size was a bit exaggerated, the sentiment was not.

Though he began the season hitting a few awe-inspiring home runs, his batting average was still slow-developing. However, by June 7, Luke had run his average up to a .309, good for fourth on the team at the time, trailing only Luis Marquez (.377), Eddie 'Pepper' Young (.365, formerly of the Chicago American Giants), and Bob Thurman (.314).[34]

Easter plagued pitchers all summer long. Jim Colzie, ace of the Indianapolis Clowns, notoriously had a tough time getting Easter out. "(You) had to throw him high and hard," Colzie later explained, "I got one low in Terre Haute one night, and the damn thing was still going up when it left the park at the 375' sign."[35]

The Grays would have an admirable 1947 campaign, but would ultimately miss the Negro League World Series for a second straight year. According to a later report, Easter hit ten home runs and batted .300 in roughly 60 league games. "No official records were kept of the 100 or more engagements the Grays played with independent outfits that summer," but counting all contests played, Easter can be credited with a season total of 43 home runs and a .382 percentage at the plate.[36]

That winter, Easter married Mildred Bethune of Pittsburgh, whom he possibly met while playing with the Grays that season. The newly-weds honeymooned in Caracas, Venezuela, where the bridegroom participated in the winter league, picking up a good amount of Spanish along the way. [37][38]

Naturally, he led the entire league in home runs that winter for his team, Patriotas de Venenzuela.[39]

# 5.

# The Negro Leagues

*"One time he hit a home run...came home, looked at me and said, 'I'm the greatest, ain't I?' That was Luke."*[1]

-Frazier 'Slow' Robinson, catcher, Baltimore Elite Giants

Though most of the attention and focus of breaking the baseball color barrier was dedicated to Robinson and to a (far) lesser degree Doby, 1947 was still paved by several other trailblazers. The St. Louis Browns, one of Easter's hometown teams, became the first team with two black players on their team, as Hank Thompson and Willard Brown debuted on July 17 and 19, 1947 respectively. Both players were veterans of the Kansas City Monarchs. On August 26, Dan Bankhead from the Memphis Red Sox broke through with the Brooklyn Dodgers as well.[2,3]

By the end of the 1947 season, three teams had integrated rosters; the Cleveland Indians, St. Louis Browns, and the Brooklyn Dodgers.

On March 25, 1948, the Homestead Grays left for spring training in Daytona Beach, Florida, picking up exhibition games along the way. "With long-ball-hitter Luke Easter in left, Louis Marquez, the NNL batting champion in center and the hard-hitting Bob Thurman and Chinky Fields alternating in right Vic (manager Victor Harris) feels that his outfield problems will be few,"[4] the local paper boasted of the talented Grays outfield.

After compiling an 11-3 record for their spring seasoning[5], the 1947 season was slated to begin for the Grays on April 28, scheduled to collide with the Baltimore Elite Giants for an evening affair at Hudson Field in Dayton, Ohio.[6] Charles Bell, a lefty offseason acquisition who accumulated a 27-1 the season before with the Lakeland Tigers in the Florida League, got the ball to start.[7] They would prevail 8-3, but no box score was available after the bout.

The Grays next contests came in the form of exhibition games the following week. They dispatched the Chicago White Sox farmhands the Oil City Refiners of the Middle-Atlantic League 12-6. Easter would go three-for-five with a double, triple, home run, and four runs batted in.[8] The Grays also played the Uniontown Coal Barons, an affiliate of the Pittsburgh Pirates, two days later.[9]

By the end of May, the Grays had run their overall record to 11-6, good enough for first place in the Negro National League. Easter's batting average sat at .344.[10]

By the middle of the summer, Easter's reputation for blasting lone home runs preceded him at nearly every stop. *The Dayton Herald* out of Dayton, Ohio, enticed would-be spectators to the ballpark with the probability of seeing an 'Easter Parade':

> "There's a possibility that 'Easter Parade' will be seen at Hudson Field tonight as well as at a downtown theater.
>
> That, of course would the parade of Luscious Luke Easter around the baselines after belting the apple out of the orchard. It's a habit the Negro slugger frequently has displayed here; so frequently, in fact, that when the Cleveland Buckeyes stopped him July 9 it was the first time he ever had failed to get at least one homer in a game at the West Side park."[11]

The clever writer was referencing the 1948 Irving Berlin film of the same name, starring Fred Astaire and Judy Garland, playing at the local cinema.

Fred Wilson of the *Delaware County Daily Times* paper also marveled at the raw power he observed of Easter at a game that summer:

"We doubt if you will see two harder hit balls than Lucious 'Luke' Easter, of the Homestead Grays, smacked down at Lloyd Field in the game with the New York Cubans on Monday (July 19, 1948) evening.

Easter poled one over the right field fence only five from the home-run marker. The ball was deep enough to have been a home run in almost any park in the majors. His single to right was hit so sharply to the right fielder that a runner on first base was almost forced at second by the throw to the infield.

Easter did not have a strike against him in five times at bat. He was walked three times on four pitches, twice intentionally, and got his two hits on the first ball near the plate each time. Sunday at the Polo Grounds he hit a 485-foot homer against the Cubans."[12][13]

Bugle Field was another venue Easter had built a fair amount of lore over his two seasons with the Grays. The field was the home of the Baltimore Elite Giants, and was a common venue for the Grays to play when they came to town. The field's dimensions, particularly in centerfield, would have certainly been, euphemistically-speaking, considered spacious. "...and 'dead' center was just what it was, a graveyard for fly balls," Elite Giants catcher Frazier 'Slow' Robinson later wrote. Though no newspaper account seems to exist, Robinson opined that Easter hit a ball when playing for the Grays that cleared the centerfield fence, 'he must have hit it pretty close to 600 feet.'[14]

On July 11, 1948, Easter's old friend and teammate Sam 'The Jet' Jethroe was signed by the Brooklyn Dodgers. He would be traded after spending the season in the minors to the Boston Braves.[15] He had been playing for the Cleveland Buckeyes of the Negro American League the previous seven seasons, winning the World Series with them in 1943.[16]

In late August, the inaugural Negro League All-Star was slated to play once more at Yankee Stadium. Given his alleged 485-foot blast at the Polo Grounds earlier in the season, it was no wonder he was chosen as the player to be prominently displayed on the game's promotional posters.[17]

The poster also included anticipated lineups as well, certainly a veritable 'who's who' for the year in Negro baseball.

In addition to Easter being tabbed as the left fielder, the Negro National League team also included teammates Buck Leonard (first base) and Luis Marquez (centerfield). The Baltimore Elite Giants were represented by James Gillam (second base), Thomas Butts (shortstop), and pitchers Robert Romby and Joe Black. The New York Cubans boasted four all-stars: Orestes Minoso ('Minnie', third base), Louis Louden (catcher), and pitchers David Barnhill and Pat Scantlebury. Right fielder Robert Harvey and pitcher Maxwell Manning represented the Newark Eagles. The Philadelphia Stars' lone representative would be catcher William Cash.[18]

The National League team would ultimately upend the American League 6-1 in front of 17,928 spectators. Gray Luis Marquez hit a two-run home run to pace the squad's offense. A moment of silence was held before the game to honor Babe Ruth, the home run king, who had passed away a week earlier.[19]

The 1948 edition of the Negro League World Series would begin about a month after the All-Star game. In 58 official league games, the Grays notched a 38-20 record, good for a .655 winning percentage and holding off the Baltimore Elite Giants (.634 winning percentage). On the American League side, the Birmingham Black Barons sporting a 55-21 regular season record (.724), had clichéd their spot. Birmingham had an up-and-comer of their own in their ranks, found in the young rookie named Willie Mays.[20]

The series got under way on September 26 in Kansas City. On the back of a three-run second inning, the Grays scored a 3-2 victory en route to a 1-0 series lead. Game two was played in Memphis, Tennessee, where the Grays notched yet another win, this time by a 5-3 score. Birmingham earned their first victory of the series in Birmingham the following day, closing the series gap to 2-1.[21]

After only 11 runs in the first three games, the Grays offense exploded in the fourth game of the series, completely routing the Black Barons 14-1 in New Orleans. The pummeling was accentuated by an Easter grand slam in the fourth inning. Though a 10-inning affair, the Grays would win game five 10-6, finishing off the Black Barons four-games-to-one, giving the franchise their first World Series title since 1944.[22]

Within league play, Easter hit .361, with 13 home runs. According to the Grays, when considering out-of-league and exhibition games that season, Easter's home run total swelled to 56 and batting average to .416.[23]

Though exuberant on the heels of a league title, it's possible that some of the Grays (and certainly many of the league's executives) were coming to a realization; their hallowed league was slowly dying. The 1948 Negro World Series would prove to be the last one ever played, and it was not given much press, even in the participant's home markets. The *Pittsburgh Courier*'s coverage after the series' final game was just a couple paragraphs long. As historian Lawrence Hogan noted:

> "The entry of additional black players in the white major and minor leagues led to the virtual abandonment of the Negro leagues by the black press...while the black papers chronicled Jackie Robinson's every move and noted the at-bats of each black player in the majors in boldface type, they began to ignore the Negro leagues."[24]

Immediately after the 1948 season, the New York Black Yankees, who lost $25,000 during their 8-32 season, closed up shop after 17 years.[25] Citing financial loss, the Cleveland Buckeyes were moved to Louisville (though they would also fold after the following season).[26]

On September 9, Effa Manley, owner of the Newark Eagles, put the team up for sale.[27] The entire Negro National League would end up folding. The Grays, after originally planning to fold and with no league to compete in, committed themselves to barnstorming the entire 1949 season.

Black ballplayers continued to be plucked from various Negro leagues through the 1948 season. Jackie Robinson and Larry Doby, who broke the color barriers in their respective leagues in 1947, both began the 1948 campaign in starting roles for the Dodgers and Indians. In April, catcher Roy Campanella debuted for the Dodgers. In July, the legendary Satchel Paige was signed by the Indians.[28] Both Doby and Paige would play substantial roles in the 1948 World Series championship run by the Indians; Doby would hit .301 in 121 games and Paige would notch a 6-1 record in 21 appearances.[29]

Though a seismic step in social history and progress, the integration of Major League Baseball was met with a fair amount of trepidation among the brain trust of the Negro leagues. At a press conference regarding the sale of her team, Manley sent verbal barbs to Branch Rickey (the Dodgers executive who spearheaded the Jackie Robinson signing) and black baseball fans themselves, stating that 'the gullibility and stupidity of Negro baseball fans...in believing that he (Rickey) has been interested in anything other than the clicking of turnstiles.' Having lost her best player, Doby, the year before, cited that 'the inferiority complex of Negros... [Since] white teams have put their stamp of approval' on black players, black baseball had been deserted.[30] A finite lifespan had clearly been set for the proud institution of black baseball leagues across the country.

As he traditionally did, Easter found work playing ball in the offseason; this time in the Puerto Rican Winter League. He was joined by teammate Wilmer Fields, and other black stars, including Dan Bankhead (of the Dodgers), Willard Brown and Artie Wilson.[31] Easter hit .402 and won the league Most Valuable Player honors for his team, the pennant-winning Mayaguez Indians.[32] In the annals of the Puerto Rican Winter League, the 1948-49 Mayaguez team is largely considered one of the best ever. Afterwards, the now-established slugger was looking for his next go-round.

Easter found himself at something of a crossroads. The writing was on the wall; teams preferred younger black players who hadn't hit their physical or ball playing peak yet for their big league clubs. As a testament to this fact, Jackie Robinson was 28, Roy Campanella was 26 when they made their debut with the Dodgers, Larry Doby was 23 when he broke through with the Indians, and Hank Thompson was 21 with the Browns. One of the lone exceptions was Satchel Paige, someone equally dodgy about age as Easter (turns out, he was 41 years old in 1948 when he made his debut). Paige had what Easter didn't in spades, a household name and box office drawing power.

Age is one of those attributes Easter was fairly elusive about during his years as a ballplayer. When looking at his career trajectory, it was hard to lay much blame. His seasons with the Titanium Giants were good to him, but a semi-pro factory baseball team would have been hardly befitting of a player with his amount of natural talent. Now, with his age 30, 31, and 32 seasons spent with the Cincinnati Crescents and Homestead Grays, Easter was more than curious about what his future prospects were. Going back to the vanishing institution of the Negro League was no longer an option, but what Major League Baseball team would gamble on a 33-year old ballplayer when there were hundreds of younger, and cheaper black prospects?

In January of 1949, the New York Giants signed Monte Irvin, the excellent outfielder and first baseman, away from the Newark Eagles.[33]

The next signing would hit very close to Easter. In the first week of February, Easter's former Grays teammate Luis Marquez was scooped up by the New York Yankees, but not without drama. Allegedly, the Cleveland Indians owner Bill Veeck believed that his club owned the option on the 23-year old Marquez, and was entitled to purchase his services. It wouldn't be the last time that Veeck and Yankees General Manager George Weiss would cross paths on the talent recruitment trail. Either way, Marquez ended up a Yankee.[34]

Veeck, competitive as ever, kept scouring for talent to better his defending champion club. Refusing defeat to a rival American League club, Veeck flew down to San Juan, Puerto Rico to do some additional scouting himself, mostly of the slick-fielding shortstop Artie Wilson, and towering first baseman Easter.

On February 9, 1949, Veeck met with Artie Wilson in Puerto Rico and offered him a contract, to which Wilson accepted. 'Our scouts say he is the best prospect in the Negro Leagues today,' Veeck said. "Better, even, than Larry Doby."[35] At the time, Wilson was also being heavily pursued by the Yankees (the Indians deal was ultimately nixed in May after the Yankees successfully argued that the Black Barons team owner had already accepted a contract offer from Weiss and the Yankees before Veeck had flown to meet Wilson). [36]

With all-star shortstop Phil Rizzuto already on the Yankees roster, why would the Yankees want Wilson? Simple, to keep him from the Indians. The arms race was on. The Yankees and the Indians spent the week crisscrossing the island, trying to steal prospects from under each other's noses; Veeck for the Indians, scout Tom Greenwade for the Yankees.[37]

Hoping to return to Cleveland with yet another prized prospect, Veeck set out to find Easter. "Since he was out of town that day and I was due back in Cleveland, I left word for our scout on the islands to start preliminary negotiations with the big fellow upon his return," Veeck later stated.

Within a couple days, representatives of the Indians were holed up with Easter in his hotel room, discussing contractual details. On February 19, 1949, Luke Easter agreed to terms with the Indians; a $10,000 contract for the year. $5,000 would be paid up front, $5,000 more if he made good with the minor league club. Easter was a now a Cleveland Indian. Veeck later recalled the process of signing Easter:

> "It happened this way...Abe Saperstein, who has known or hired every outstanding Negro athlete for the past 20 years, has been a close friend of mine for about the same period. Ever since

Easter made good with the Crescents, Abe had been writing and speaking to me about him. I saw Luke play for the first time in the East-West All-Star Negro game...back in 1948. He clouted a couple that day that are still going. Just before I took off to sign Wilson, I happened to be talking to Abe on the phone. 'Don't forget to take another look at Easter,' were his parting words to me."[38]

When the team asked how old the 33-year old was, Easter answered that he was 27 without hesitation, obviously not wanting his deal to go south on account of his advanced age.

Easter was to report to Ontario, California for the San Diego Padres spring training (the Indians triple-A affiliate) of the Pacific Coast League early the next month.

*Though Bill Veeck had hard-earned his reputation as showman, he worked diligently to smoothly integrate baseball. Shown here in a 1944 Marine Corps-issued photo. (Public Domain)*

# 6.

## The Coastal Phenom

*"I wish they'd get him out of here before he kills every infielder in the Coast League."*[1]

-*Hollywood Stars Manager Fred Haney when asked how he felt about the meteoric rise of Luke Easter.*

Heading into spring training for the 1949 season, Bill Veeck and the Cleveland Indians looked like the most progressive team in the league, as 14 black ballplayers were spread throughout the organization. Aside from Satchel Paige and Larry Doby on the big league team, Artie Wilson, Minnie Minoso (who was actually born in Cuba), and Easter were the prospects with the highest profile. "To my estimation," Jesse Butler of the *Cleveland Call and Post* wrote "Bill Veeck of the Cleveland Indians did more for the Negro than any man last year. His liberalism and giving Negroes a chance to show their real ability as major leaguers spearhead the attack on racial discrimination and segregation in this country."[2]

Veeck, though portrayed as something of a showman in the mainstream media (to be fair, a persona he certainly earned and would continue to earn), proved to be a positive force in the pre-civil rights movement America. Upon arriving in Cleveland, he joined the local chapter of the National Association for the Advancement of Colored People (NAACP) and was an enthusiastic supporter, even appearing on a recruiting poster for the organization with Doby and Paige.[3]

These efforts were truly not a publicity gambit for Veeck. He had been trying to buy a Major League Baseball franchise for years, starting in 1942 with an attempt to buy the bankrupt Philadelphia Phillies. He had every intention on bolstering the seventh place club with players of color. Word was, once Commissioner

Kennesaw Mountain Landis, a longtime proponent of segregated baseball, heard of the plan he nixed the deal. Not to be defeated, Veeck ended up settling for purchasing the Milwaukee Brewers, then a minor league team. While attending a spring training game in Ocala, Florida, Veeck emerged from the owner's box and sat in the 'Colored Only' section of the bleachers. The mayor and the local sheriff quickly converged and threatened to kick him out of the game. Veeck threatened to take his entire spring operation out of Ocala. Veeck prevailed, and sat with the blacks in attendance.[4] Safe to say, the occasion would have probably marked the first time a team owner of a white club would have been found in that particular section of seating.

Unlike nearly every Major League Baseball owner and executive at the time (including Branch Rickey), Veeck would *purchase* the contracts of his players from Negro League teams, offering teams like the Newark Eagles, Homestead Grays, and the Kansas City Monarchs compensation in return for the players he would sign away from them. Nearly all other black players were signed as free agents with no money being exchanged between their parent Negro League club and their new Major League Baseball club, with executives citing the reserve clause in many Negro League contracts.[5]

For a bit of seasoning, Easter was assigned to the San Diego Padres spring training camp in Ontario, California. Shortly after reporting, team president Bill Starr warned Easter of the prejudice he might encounter, being the second black player in the Pacific Coast League, after teammate Johnny Ritchey. Easter wasn't worried, 'Mr. Starr,' he allegedly affirmed, "Everybody likes me when I hit the ball."[6] *The Sporting News* reported the same exchange quite differently, fashioning Easter's response to Starr as "Mistuh, when ah hits dat home run ball, everybody likes me."[7] This type of coverage and personification of Easter would become increasingly frequent in the coming years.

Not everyone within the Indians organization was sold on the big slugger as immediately as Veeck was. Indians Vice President Hank Greenberg made a special trip to the Padres spring training camp in Ontario, expressly to watch the new acquisition. He brought the Indians West Coast lead scout Hollis Thurston along with him. The two were admitted skeptics of Easter. As they were walking across the diamond during batting practice the first morning of spring training, Easter came up to bat to take his first swings as a Padre. "He swung at the first ball pitched to him," Thurston recalled later, "And it traveled at least 450 feet. It was the longest drive I had ever seen at that park. Hank looked at me and didn't say a thing. He just grinned."[8]

The inclinations of Greenberg and Thurston looked accurate early in camp, as Easter made an immediate splash. "Big Lucius (Luke) Easter stole the show in today's drill, the giant Negro driving the ball to all corners of the field – and far – as he reported for his first workout," the *Los Angeles Times* reported on March 6. "Easter, batting left-handed, looked as impressive against curveballs as he did against fast ones. Manager Bucky Harris placed Easter at first after watching Luke smack a couple to the centerfield wall, 425 feet away."[9]

At their March 8 exhibition against the Sacramento Solons, also of the Pacific Coast League, Easter was penciled in to bat fifth and play first base. With Greenberg in attendance, Easter would go two-for-three with an RBI single in the third and a two-run home run in the fifth, pacing the team to a 8-2 victory.[10] Two days later, two "towering" triples and a sacrifice fly netted him three more RBI against the Seattle Rainiers in a 9-5 victory.[11] On March 12, again against Seattle, Easter hit yet another home run, complemented by two singles and three runs.[12]

Easter was making quite an impression on the field during spring training, as was his style off the field.

"Brother Easter has to be seen to be appreciated," wrote Frank Finch of *The Los Angeles Times*, "His shoulders are so broad that when he wears one of his racy pinstripe suits you think, at first glance, that he forgot to remove the coat hanger." Finch continued, "Easter's a St. Louis boy, and he's just as much of a showboat as the old sidewheelers that used to steam up and down the Mississippi. He sports a diamond ring that looks like the headlight on the Santa Fe Chief...Luke is also the owner of the longest and loudest Buick that's built – one of those racy models with four portholes on each side amidships."[13]

Easter loved to be the center of attention. He would even occasionally ask teammate Artie Wilson "to act as his chauffeur and let him sit in the back seat so that when he was driving around town people would think a big shot was passing by."[14]

The car was part of Luke's larger-than-life persona. So much so that *The Sporting News* felt compelled to report that after buying the Buick, Luke hit his first pitch in batting practice the following day 425 feet. Later that afternoon, in a game against Sacramento, he hit another home run that drove in three runs.[15]

Wilson would be returned to the Yankees in May, after the details of his signing dispute were finally settled. With no other black players to room with in Oakland, the hot-tempered, future Yankee skipper Billy Martin volunteered to be his roommate. "Billy Martin didn't have a prejudiced bone in his body. He was a super guy."[16] Wilson later wrote.

Bucky Harris, Padres manager (who had managed the New York Yankees the previous two seasons, winning a World Series in 1947) handed Easter the first base job after turning in a .407 (24-59) batting average for the spring.[17]

On the eve of the regular season's commencement, the Padres entertained the defending champion Indians for a final exhibition game. During the game, Larry Doby crashed into Easter at first base after rapping out a hit and rounding the base. Both were shaken up and checked on by one of the team trainers, Lefty Weisman.[18] Most of the attention was on Doby, who even at six feet, one inch, 180 pounds was utterly dwarfed by Easter, and most would have assumed that Doby bore the brunt of the collision. After Easter stood up, he immediately felt an incredibly sharp pain in his right knee.

After Weisman returned to the dugout, Doby continued to pace around the field, stretching, ensuring himself he could continue. During the entire aftermath of the episode, Easter stood almost completely still, unable to move. He insisted he was also fine and play continued. Not seeing any other recourse, Easter played on, not initially telling a soul the severity of his pain. He would find out later that the collision had broken his kneecap.

When the Padres took to Lane Field in San Diego on March 30 for Opening Day, the San Diego Padres would become the first professional baseball team to boast three black players in their starting nine. Easter started at first base and batted fifth, the slick-fielding Artie Wilson started at shortstop and led off the order, and Johnny Ritchie (who broke the PCL color barrier the previous season) was behind the plate and batting seventh.[19]

The high temperature that day was 62 degrees, and rain was imminent. Perhaps due to the pending weather (rain would begin in the second inning and wouldn't let up), the pregame ceremony was "mercifully brief" according to Finch, *The Los Angeles Times* beat writer. As a result, the crowd was a fairly disappointing 4,580. The game would be called after play was halted twice, stuck in a 3-3 deadlock. "Even Donald Duck would have been driven to the showers tonight," opined Finch. Easter, in his Pacific Coast League debut, would single twice and drive in a run.[20]

After going homerless the first three games of the regular season, he proceeded to hit circuit clouts his next three games. "Easter Paces Coast Batsmen" the newspapers proclaimed. After six games Easter was sporting a .500 batting average, going 11-22. The mark led the league for players who had played in all six contests. His three home runs and 10 RBI also led the league.[21]

The excitement surrounding Easter that had been building between spring training and the first week of the PCL regular season had hit a critical mass. The relative unknown had taken the entire league by storm.

Spectators flooded to the ballpark to see Easter by the tens of thousands. The demand for the slugger was as such that Starr began ordering special batting practice exhibitions before each home game, with Easter as the lone attraction. Fans would arrive at the field two, sometimes three hours early, line the fence, even standing on the hoods of their cars to peer over the stadium walls, whatever it took to see the improbable, impossibly long home runs that jumped off the bat of the rookie Easter. Just as Easter had when he was a boy at Cardinals and Browns games, children would congregate around the cracks in the stadium fences, trying to catch a glimpse of the slugger. Among the spectators was a black teenager from Oakland, Frank Robinson. Robinson would go on to have a Hall of Fame playing career and eventually become the first black manager in baseball history. "He was awesome...I was amazed by his strength and power." Robinson later remembered.[22]

20,000 or more fans routinely packed into stadiums to watch the contests. Finch, this time lending his words to *The Sporting News*, reported:

> "When he takes his turn at batting practice, the other players, goober salesmen, and fans rivet their eyes on the batting cage to watch Luke powder the ball with a free-wheeling southpaw swing that's smooth as silk. I've seen only three other batters paid that singular compliment – Ted Williams, Stan Musial and Ernie Lombardi."[23]

Luke Easter as a box office draw was in full effect. PCL executives entered the 1949 with an expectation that attendance would drop 20%, due to the vague explanation of the "general tightening up of business...but the sag hasn't materialized yet," Al Wolf of the *Los Angeles Times* noted, "In fact, attendance has been picking up with warmer weather – and an ever-warmer Luke Easter."[24]

The profile of Luke Easter, in the course of less than a month, found dozens of major newspapers across the country following his exploits with the Padres daily. Gordon Graham, a sportswriter from Lafayette, Indiana, who had watched Easter punish local semi-pro teams as a member of the Crescents, marveled at the talent of Easter, a talent he'd been exposed to years prior, while lamenting at the unfair system black players had been subjected to up to that point in his (nearly) daily essay titled 'Graham Crackers' for the *Journal and Courier*:

> "Sometimes it is difficult to feel sorry for several of the major league clubs which operate on 'short dough' against the money bag teams...certainly the Sox, the Browns, the Senators, or some team other than Bill Veeck and the Cleveland Indians could have picked up Luke Easter, the giant Negro first baseman, who is packing the fans in the park for San Diego in the Pacific Coast League these days...here was a huge 6-4, 220 pound Negro could run...not only that, he could clout the ball a mile...a lefthanded hitter, Easter walloped a couple clear across East Main street, while playing with the Cincinnati Crescents...three years of hitting over .350 and showering home runs all over the land, wasn't enough to earn him a tumble...Easter had to keep up his slugging in a winter league south of the border before Cleveland finally took hold."[25]

On the exact day of Graham's Lafayette musings, one of the first public questionings of Easter's age arose in *Oakland Tribune*. "Luke Says It Was 1921", a reference to the year Easter insisted was that of his birth. The challenge proved to be a fairly passive one, with the write-up opting to spend a large portion on Easter's philosophy on striking out: "The toughest thing to do in baseball, Luke has discovered, is to strike out. He means that two ways. First, it's not often that a pitcher can get three strikes by him. Second, if he does fan he takes it 'mighty hard'."[26]

In mid-May, Minnie Minoso headed west to join the Padres, seeing as he was not getting consistent at-bats with the big league club in Cleveland. Shortly after his arrival, he, like Easter, was called in for a chat with the team president Bill Starr. He was given a distinctly different pep talk than Easter was. "You are a nice, young fellow,' Starr said. 'I don't want you hanging around Luke Easter. I don't want you getting his bad habits." Minoso took note, but also didn't always follow the advice. When the team was in Hollywood to play the Stars, Easter asked Minoso to accompany him to a theater to see a Western film playing, but then proceeded to stay out all night. 'We play a doubleheader the next day," Minoso recalled, "Luke got 4-for-5. I am begging God, but I only get 1-for-5. I know Mr. Starr is right. I say to Luke, 'I love you. You are my friend, but I can't keep up with you.'"[27]

Easter, pairing with fellow power hitter, and former big leaguer Max West, gave the Padres the most potent middle-of-the-orders in the entire PCL. By the end of May, Easter was leading all hitters with a .400 batting average through 57 games (74-185). This included 18 home runs and 67 RBI. West had accumulated a .299 average (63-211), swatting 20 home runs and driving in 70 runs. The team sat in second place with a 35-28 record.[28]

With the Indians mired in a slump in Cleveland, particularly offensively, there was a panic that Easter's time in the circuit would be limited, for fear of his being called up to the big leagues. "Personally, we're keeping our fingers crossed." Wolf wrote for the *Times,* "Because 'characters' are all too few in the PCL and any ending to the Easter parade would be a bruising blow, indeed, not only to the Padres but to the entire loop."[29]

Easter was wildly popular and had become the toast of the Pacific Coast League, but he was not exonerated from the racially-charged actions that season. As historian Jules Tygiel wrote, "In the age of Jim Crow, common stereotypes had depicted black ballplayers as road-show clowns, far inferior to their white counterparts. The high standards established by baseball's racial pioneers (such as Easter) created a new, no less stereotypical, image of the black athlete." Tygiel continued "Americans readily assimilated the new image of blacks. As 'natural' athletes, blacks depended on brawn and reflex rather than brain or reason..."[30]

Easter himself was consistently subjected to being depicted with 'Stepin Fetchit' mannerisms and way of speak. For instance, *The Sporting News* quoted Easter saying phrases such as 'I shore likes to play and I likes the money I'm making'.[31] Easter was also quoted 'Ah'm the type o' gentulman which feels embarrassed if, with the bases loaded, ah don't get a hit!' In a later piece, a cartoon of Easter was published, this time approaching former St. Louis Cardinal Pepper Martin, of whom he would have certainly been a fan of. The fat-lipped caricature of Easter exclaimed,

'Mistah Peppah Mahtin! May Ah I have yo' autograff?'[32] Though it was certainly not the way Easter spoke, it was often how he was portrayed; slow-witted, with an often indistinguishable Southern dialect.

Easter, being one of the few blacks in the PCL, and given his propensity to hit tape measure home runs, was frequently targeted by brush back pitches and bean balls. A month into the season league president Clarence Rowland, in response to complaints about pitches aimed at Easter, issued a memorandum to all the teams in the league regarding the usage of the bean ball directed at Easter and his black teammates. Early in the season, 42-year old Portland pitcher Ad Liska, a 24-year veteran, threw behind Easter twice in a single at-bat. Easter responded with a towering home run followed by a line drive single back through the box (allegedly narrowly missing Liska himself) the next two times up.[33]

Easter had been performing at an incredibly high level, at his reputation was proceeding him at every stop, even with a bad knee. However, his issues were aggravated when he was hit square on the problematic right kneecap by a fastball sometime in early June.[34]

On June 12, it was reported that he might be in need of a knee operation. Easter continued to play through the pain for an additional week or so until being flown out to see the Indians medical team on June 24. X-rays disclosed what Easter had probably known all season; he had suffered, and been playing on, a chipped kneecap. On July 2, Easter's right knee was operated on at the Cleveland Clinic by Dr. James Dickson. An inch-long bone chip was removed from his joint. He was expected to be sidelined at least five weeks.[35]

Easter's tenure, and what could only be described as almost a mythical summer in San Diego, was over after less than four months.

He left an indelible mark on the Pacific Coast League, leading the entire circuit in batting average upon his exit with a mark of .363. Factoring in the 45 walks he took, his on-base percentage ballooned to a robust .460. All told, in 80 games, Easter would record 99 hits, 25 home runs (second in the league, trailing only teammate West's, 27 at the time) and 92 RBI, which led the league when he departed.[36]

For the movement of baseball's integration, Easter (and his black teammates) deserve much of the credit. "History cannot ignore the fact that Big Luke was an important contributor to the cause of integration." A.S. 'Doc' Young wrote in *Jet Magazine*, "His most important donation was proof that when an athlete hits home runs and plays a Titanic game, fans quickly lose sight of his color."[37] When the 1949 season began, the Padres were the only integrated PCL club, By the end of July, there were a total of nine black players on four different clubs.[38]

Easter's loss was temporarily crippling for the PCL. Attendance, as Al Wolf had feared, plummeted quickly. Team owners said the loss of Easter had cost them $200,000 in gate receipts.[39]

Easter pushed the rehabilitation of his right knee as strenuously as he could while recovering in Cleveland. He wanted to get back to playing as soon as possible.

38 days after his operation, Easter worked out with the Indians before they played the St. Louis Browns on August 9. It was his first complete workout in over a month; he jogged around the field for a bit, and took some pitches for batting practice. After the session, Owner Veeck and President Hank Greenberg were publicly non-committal about whether Easter would be sent back to San Diego, or if he would stay in Cleveland with the big league club.[40]

Internally, their conversations would have been markedly different. Though Veeck's defending champion club was sitting at a 61-43 mark, the team remained 4.5 games behind the New York Yankees atop the American League. The Indians 463 runs scored were third-worst in the entire league, and 140 runs behind the league-leading Boston Red Sox.[41] It was clear that they could certainly use an offensive spark, particularly in the form of the long ball (no Indian would end the season with more than Doby's 24 home runs- only one other Indian eclipsed the 20-mark). If

Easter arrived as advertised, that need could be addressed, short order.

The following day, August 11, it was decided; Luke Easter was going to stay in Cleveland and join the Indians. The slugger with a still-sore knee was being counted on for the Indians offense down the pennant stretch. Popular outfielder Alfred 'Allie' Clark was optioned to San Diego, and Easter took his roster spot.[42] From the onset, Manager Lou Boudreau's plan was to mostly use Easter as a pinch hitter while his right knee healed. The Indians, desperate to overtake the powerful Yankees, were hoping to catch a bit of lightning in a bottle with the injured slugger down the stretch.[43]

Though wildly improbable from the onset, the 34-year old Luke Easter was about to become a Major League Baseball player.

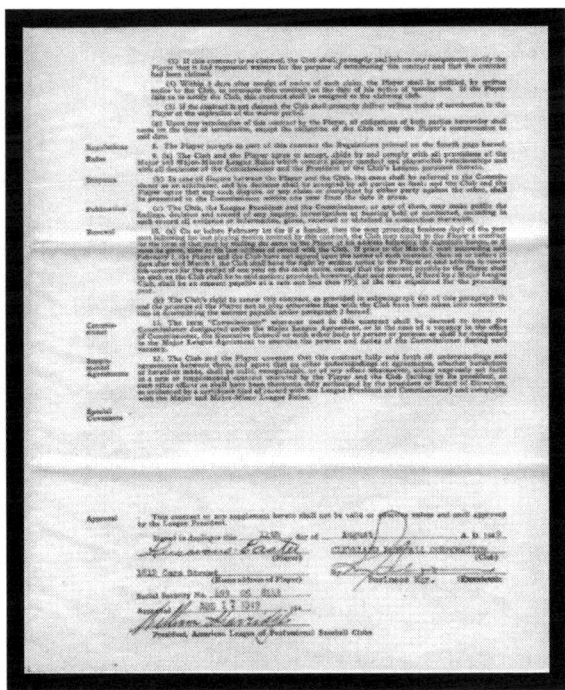

*The final page of Easter's contract when the team purchased his rights from San Diego. (Cleveland Indians team archives)*

# 7.

# A (Bitter) Cup of Coffee

*"Luke's been kicking around longer than he admits, I think...I am afraid he is too old to learn the fine points of big league ball..."*

*Anonymous 'Guest Expert', from an Associated Press December, 1949 feature.*

A 'cup of coffee' is baseball parlance for a short time spent in the Major Leagues. The expression is applicable in a couple different scenarios; a cup of coffee can be a young, or new prospect who is getting some time with the big league club late in the season as something of an audition, or it could also extend to a player serving as organizational depth, getting the call to plug an unexpected hole due to an injury or some other circumstance.

When Easter joined the Indians, set to get his cup of coffee, in mid-August of 1949, there were only seven other black ballplayers in the majors. Two of whom were teammates, Larry Doby and Satchel Paige. The Brooklyn Dodgers featured Jackie Robinson, Roy Campanella, and Don Newcombe. The New York Giants listed Hank Thompson and Monte Irvin among their regulars.[2] The Indians were already the first American League team to integrate. They were now the first American League team with three black players on the squad.

Little time was wasted in getting Easter acclimated or eased into life as a major leaguer; he was put on the active roster immediately after being told he was staying in Cleveland. When asked by the *Cleveland Plain Dealer* how it felt to be in the big leagues, he responded 'It sure does feel good. I hopes (sic) to do some awful good hitting, because my knee feels a lot better.'[3] The statement, while hopeful, was actually rather far from the truth. Easter, sidelined and inactive for over five weeks (save for throwing the commemorative first pitch at the Indians game on August 1)[4], reported to the Indians at 256 pounds, almost 20 pounds heavier than his usual playing weight.[5] Save a few exhibitions, he had never faced big league pitching either.

When meeting with Indians head trainer Wally Bock to have his knees examined, Easter was laid up on the examination table. Bock, upon inspecting Easter's maligned knees whispered, "I can feel your bones. I know how old you are."

"Please don't tell anybody," pleaded Easter, in a rare moment of external vulnerability.[6]

When Easter was set to make his debut, the Indians were faced with three issues: first, a nearly-five game deficit in the standings separated themselves and the Yankees. Second, despite great pitching, the team's overall offensive efforts had been fairly lackluster for most of the season. Finally, and of great consequence, the team was averaging four thousand less fans in the seats per game than the previous season. 'Big Luke' was expected to assist in fixing all three issues in one fell swoop.

The second place Indians were slated to play the sixth-place Chicago White Sox at home that Thursday, August 11 day. The 25-year old Mike Garcia, one of the few Hispanic players in the league, was given the ball to start for the Indians. Garcia, sporting a 9-4 record heading into the game, would ultimately lead the entire American League in earned run average that season.[7]

The game started poorly for the Indians. Garcia was bounced after allowing three runs in only two innings. Cleveland would answer back, scoring two runs in the bottom of the second, cutting the deficit to 3-2. By the bottom of the 8$^{th}$ inning, the score stood 5-3 in favor of the Sox. After starting the inning with hits from Joe Gordon and Johnny Berardino, outfielder Bob Kennedy drove them both home with a sharp single, advancing to second on the throw. With the score tied, Mike Tresh grounded out to move Kennedy to third with one out. With pitcher Sam Zoldak projected to hit next, Manager Lou Boudreau made the decision to call on his new lefty, Luke Easter, for pinch-hitting duties.[8]

Easter swung three bats while standing in the on-deck circle, including a lead-filled weighted bat, as was his routine. Despite being cleared for baseball activities (probably fueled his own persistence), Easter still sported a noticeable limp in his gait while walking up to the plate. As he made his way to the left-handed batter's box, Easter "brought a gasp from the dumbfounded spectators."[9] This could have been the result of the size of Easter, easily the biggest player in the organization, his reputation proceeding him as the prized jewel of the Indians farm system, or possibly the sheer surprise in seeing the slugger in action so soon after his well-publicized surgery. The astonished crowd may have also been a bit starstruck in seeing the almost-fabled prospect for the first time.

With the go-ahead run standing on third base with one out, the Indians had a prime scoring opportunity. Having not faced live pitching in almost six weeks, Easter was still banging off the rust. Marino Pieretti, the diminutive righty relief pitcher, standing five foot, seven inches, and 170-pounds, faced down the massive lefty. Easter took a massive cut during the at-bat, but ultimately swung a bit late and rolled over the pitch, sending a weak ground ball to Sox shortstop Luke Appling, who easily threw Easter out at first. Kennedy, standing on third, could not score on the play. Despite the missed chance, the Indians would go on to win in 12 innings, 6-5.[10]

Other than the reaction from the home crowd, there was almost no national fanfare attached to Easter's debut. After Robinson broke into Major League Baseball a little over two years before, there was little pomp and circumstance to those who followed him by the national media (including for Doby, who followed Robinson by just a couple months). In making the appearance, history had been made: Easter had just become the 11th player in Major League Baseball to break the color barrier.

Over the next two weeks, Easter would receive six more pinch hitting opportunities, going hitless, but drawing two walks.

On August 25, pinch hitting for Bob Feller in the seventh inning of a game against the Yankees, Easter sent a sharp ground ball towards the third baseman Bobby Brown. Deflecting off Brown's glove, the ball caromed towards shortstop Phil Rizzuto. Rizzuto collected the ball and fired to first base, but Easter just beat the throw out for his first major league hit.[11]

On August 29, Boudreau, possibly being pressured by Veeck and Greenberg, announced that Easter would start for the rest of the season any time there was a right-handed starting pitcher for the opposition. With first baseman Mickey Vernon playing too well to have Easter spell him, right field was the defensive destination for the rookie. While Boudreau wouldn't admit publicly, the move was unquestionably aimed to boost Easter's confidence and to get him more regular at-bats, having gone one-for-twelve (.083 batting average) to begin his professional career.[12]

"It has been fairly obvious in recent weeks that unless the Indians can dig up some substantial additional punch their flag chances are practically non-existent," Gordon Cobbledick of the *Plain Dealer* lamented. He continued:

> "Have they dug it up on Easter? Authorities differ...You have your choice between the opinions of the grandstand wolves who like neither Easter's color nor his inconclusive performance to date and the opinion of such men as Hank Greenberg and Bucky Harris, who insist he will hit...In calling the big guy's performance inconclusive, I have in mind not only the fact that he hasn't had time to adjust to the faster tempo of the big league ball but also the fact that he is recuperating from a recent operation on an injured knee. It's tough enough to hit on two sound legs, considerably tougher on only one."

Though the Cleveland faithful seemed to be quickly, and impatiently, turning on Easter, Cobbledick maintained a "wait-and-see" approach, quick not to pin the Indians' misfortune square on the shoulders of the rookie.

> "So Easter has to do it for the Indians before he can be accepted. What he did in San Diego doesn't count. But in giving him his chance, Boudreau has everything to gain and nothing to lose. It was pretty plain that the Tribe wasn't going to win with what it had. If Easter hits it may win. If he doesn't it's no worse off than it was before his introduction in the lineup."[13]

Unfortunately for Easter, his troubles at the plate seemed to be compounding. After Cobbledick's musings on behalf of Easter, he would only notch one base hit (a single) in his next twelve plate appearances (though he would draw two base on balls). His batting average stood at a paltry .091. Cleveland Municipal Stadium filled with boos and heckles every time he came up to the plate for his turn to hit. "Few Cleveland Indians have had such a large jeering section as big as Luke Easter has come up with on recent days," the *Plain Dealer* opined. "But have you noticed how carefully opposing pitchers work on the big guy? The jeer leaders and their followers wouldn't get that."[14] Regardless of how the opposition was pitching him, Easter's cup of coffee was not going as planned.

In his entire career, the slugger had never experienced such a public slump before. Every ballplayer goes through the occasional hitting slumps, but Easter's was magnified by his unrealistically inflated expectations, paired with frustration with the team's overall performance to-date. His knee ached incredibly. His confidence and trademark dander had all but vanished, crushed under the crippling expectation of pumping lifeblood into a team with ever-dwindling pennant hopes.

By September 21, the Indians had fallen to fourth place in the American League, 10.5 games behind the Yankees. There would be no World Series for the defending champion Indians.

On that same day, the Indians readied to take on the Boston Red Sox. As Easter was standing behind the batting cage during warmups, waiting for his turn to take batting practice, an unexpected visitor started towards him for a chat: Red Sox legend

Ted Williams. Williams, easily the most famous San Diego Padres alum, walked up to Easter to offer some words of encouragement.

"You can hit the ball, Luke," Williams told him. "Take your time, relax and just belt the insides out of the ball when it comes up to you."[15]

In the fifth inning that day, with Mickey Vernon standing on first base and the Indians clinging to a 2-1 lead, Easter walked up to the plate to face off against two-time all-star Jack Kramer. Easter promptly ripped a double to right field, scoring Vernon from first (his first career extra base hit and run batted in).

Two innings later, with the Indians now trailing 6-4, Easter sent another screaming double to left field, this time off Chuck Stobbs, again scoring Vernon.

Easter would also lead off the ninth inning with a single, his third hit of the afternoon. Almost fittingly, it was Williams' seventh inning home run that would break the 6-6 tie and be the difference in the Red Sox win.[16]

The local paper claimed that Easter "had finally lived up to his advance billings."[17] Easter joked in retelling the incident, "Wish that Ted Williams could talk to me every day like that before a game."[18]

With Williams' pep talk perhaps serving as a catalyst, Easter would hit .348, with a .423 on-base percentage to close out his final six games of the season. The Indians themselves would ultimately finish third in the American League with an 89-65 record, eight games behind the eventual World Series champion Yankees. Though finishing on a high note, Easter's batting average over his time with the Indians stood at .222, with three doubles and two RBI. He did walk eight times as opposed to six strikeouts.[19]

The climate that Easter was introduced to when joining the Indians in 1949 was far from ideal. Rushed into action after surgery, with such high expectations, and mostly being relegated to a pinch hitting role (as nearly half of his appearances were) was not conducive to a high level of success on the playing field.

Hall of Famer and then-Indians coach/adviser Tris Speaker told the *Cleveland News* that Easter "Came up under the worst possible conditions. From the day he entered the stadium he was booed...Worst of all, this poor guy had absolutely nothing to do with the condition that made him a target of the boo birds."[20]

Easter would make his debut on August 11, 1949, becoming the eleventh black player to break the color barrier. He is shown here taking a swing early in his Indians tenure. (Cleveland Indians team archives)

Though the 1949 season was over, there was still plenty of activity during the offseason. As he had for the previous years, Indians ace Bob Feller collected a team of players to play barnstorming contests with. Tapping into the box office draw that was Luke Easter in the state of California, Feller's white 'Leaguers' and

Easter's black 'All-Stars' went up the coast playing each other in exhibition matchups.[21] The tour was also organized at the behest of Abe Saperstein.[22]

Prominently featured on Easter's All-Stars was Sam Bankhead of the Brooklyn Dodgers, Indians farmhands Al Smith and Harry 'Suitcase' Simpson, and even Easter's younger brother, Wilbur Easter of the St. Louis Giants. Easter handed the managerial reins over to Winfield Welch, his old skipper from the Cincinnati Crescents. Easter's team also faced-off with Philadelphia Athletic Ferris Fain's collective as well.[23]

Back in Cleveland, owner Bill Veeck was on his way out. A divorce proceeding had forced him to sell the team. Ellis Ryan, a Cleveland insurance executive, purchased the club for $2.2 million.[24] Veeck would compile a progressive record over his 41 months as owner of the Indians. When interviewed about a month after the sale was complete, Veeck was still beaming about Easter. "He'll be okay next year," Veeck assured. "Why last summer I saw him hit ball into the stands in right field...it went on a bee line out there, never more than twenty feet off the ground. I'll tell you this," Veeck said continued confidently, "I would have traded Mickey Vernon and put Luke on first as soon as he got to Cleveland. But his knee was bad and we were afraid to take the chance."[25]

Among new owner Ryan's first orders of business was installing Hank Greenberg in a new role as general manager. Greenberg nearly immediately, and publicly, backed Easter as an everyday player in the coming season despite a lackluster 1949 campaign. "Look," he patiently told reporters. "I saw Easter on the coast. I talked to people whose opinion I value – people like Del Baker and Bucky Harris. I thought the big guy was as great as anything I'd ever seen."[26]

To ready his knee for a full season, Easter spent a month in Hot Springs, Arkansas for his conditioning program. He took an old racing bike with him, and he pedaled around five miles a day to strengthen his knee. Mountain climbing was also a part of his daily workout regimen.[27]

The 1950 season would bring different expectations for Easter. He had the public vote of confidence from team management, and every newspaper in the country reported a new contract for the season signed on January 15.[28]

"I haven't seen a pitcher good enough to fool him yet." Veeck exclaimed in the aforementioned interview when offering his final thoughts on Easter. "You mark my words, Luke Easter is going to be the batting champion of the American League real soon, maybe next season."[29]

# 8.

# Breakout

*"The two most powerful men I ever saw at the plate were Babe Ruth and Luke Easter."[1]*

-Bob Feller

Easter was feeling well enough after the winter of 1949-50 that the still-rookie made a bit of a proclamation. Speaking with Al Abrams, the Sports Editor for the *Pittsburgh Post-Gazette*, he told a story about meeting Pittsburgh Pirates slugger Ralph Kiner while barnstorming the previous year, and how the two would compete head-to-head in home run competitions before games. Spliced in the conversation, Easter was direct with the expectations he had set for himself heading into the 1950 season. "I've set my goal for a .300 batting average and 25 home runs. I know the pitching is tougher up here, but I think I'll be able to handle it."[2] The *Jefferson City Post-Tribune* even added "He stands six feet four inches in his stocking feet and moves with the grace of a ballet dancer," in their flattering write-up.[3]

Easter looked sharp in spring training camp in Tucson, Arizona. For their part, his Indians teammates made the rookie feel welcome at his first big league spring training (he spent the previous spring almost exclusively with the Padres in their camp). Pitcher Gene Bearden routinely volunteered to throw Easter extra batting practice pitches. Outfielders Thurman Tucker and Larry Doby stood nearby to dispense hitting tips. Infielder Johnny Berardino often spent time with Easter after practice was over to work on his defense and throwing mechanics.[4]

In making the leap to big league pitching, the additional instruction was invaluable. Easter was a natural, but raw, hitter. He had never thought of hitting as a scientific endeavor, "It's a gift," he once recalled, "It's like a fella feels he can play the piano. I know I can hit. I feel it inside."[5]

Due to the establishment's policy, Easter, Doby and their black teammates were not permitted to stay in the Santa Rita Hotel in Tucson with the rest of the team. They would stay with the family of Chester and Lucille Willis on the west side of the city.[6] Easter was forced to shower at the team facility, since he was too large for the Willis' small bathtub.[7]

Easter and Doby shared an interesting relationship. Heading into the 1950 season, Easter and Doby would wind up being be the only black players in the American League circuit. It is assumed that they both understood the history they were making together (along with their other black teammates) in Cleveland, but Doby and Easter shared very little companionship. It didn't help that Doby and Easter were on the complete opposite ends of the personality spectrum. Doby was intense on the field; very little could break his focus from the game. Even off the field, he tended to be fairly serious most of the time. So much so, in fact, the local writers often gave Doby grief as he may have seemed aloof due to his personality. Easter was the antithesis; he was generally relaxed and tried enjoyed his status as a big league baseball player. Teammate Al Rosen later said that "Luke was a great guy, easy-going, devil-may-care, jolly...kind of guy who took a ribbing and dished it out. Larry... (I think) may have looked at Luke like an Uncle Tom type."[8]

To further illustrate the difference between the men, New York Yankees Hall-of-Fame catcher Yogi Berra shared the following anecdote in 1956:

> "Of course you got to know how far you can go with each batter. For instance catchers seldom talk to Larry Doby. Larry dislikes catchers who shoot the breeze. So I respect his moods...I used to josh the pants off Luke Easter about his feet. Whenever he'd come up to swing I'd rib him about not being able to squeeze his gunboats into

the batter's box. If I reached first on a hit or a walk, I'd make it a point to keep stepping on his toes. Of course, it was all a good-natured joke, sort of a bond between Luke and me."[9]

Perhaps Rosen may have remembered it best, stating "It was often said in our clubhouse that if you could put Larry Doby's talent with Luke Easter's outlook, you'd have the greatest player on two legs."[10]

Back in Tucson, Easter was hitting .323 (20-for-62) with five home runs and 16 runs batted in after a month of exhibition play.[11] Despite Easter being thought of as the first baseman of the future, it had become clear to the Indians brass that getting a fair trade for first baseman Mickey Vernon would be tough sledding. Therefore, Easter worked out the entire spring training in right field. But that didn't mean he didn't have any competition. Fan-favorite Alfred 'Allie' Clark, whom Easter replaced on the squad the previous August, was pushing for a starting position as well. "All I read all winter was about the big guy being the Indians right fielder," Allie said. "Luke Easter this, and Luke Easter that...What about little Alfie? I decided to report in shape. Extra weight gave me a poor start in 1949."[12] Coming in a bit slimmer, Clark had posted a .479 batting average through a month of spring training (he would ultimately make the club as a reserve).

Uncannily, for the second straight spring training, Easter would again be involved in a collision with a teammate just before the start of the regular season. On April 9, the Indians were playing an exhibition tilt against the New York Giants. Wes Westrum hit a lazy fly ball to right center. Centerfielder Bob Kennedy started in for it, as did Easter. The two collided and fell hard to the grass. In an anxiety-ridden moment, Kennedy was lying flat on his back and Easter was in a half-seated position. To the relief of everyone present, both players stood up and the game resumed. The game would be stopped again when Easter discovered he couldn't move his arm to throw after the next ball was hit his way. "He took himself out immediately, and an over-crowded press box went into frenzied action in dispatching the unexpected of the Easter Story to the baseball world." Jim Schlemmer of the *Akron Beacon*

*Journal* reported. He was diagnosed with a mild separated left shoulder. Easter also shared with Schlemmer that it was not the first time he had the same issue with a shoulder, saying "he had a left shoulder separation years ago when as a youngster in St. Louis he fell off a playground swing."[13]

Unlike the previous year, the injury wouldn't prove to be as much of a nag, as it was ensured that Easter would be ready for the start of the season nine days later.

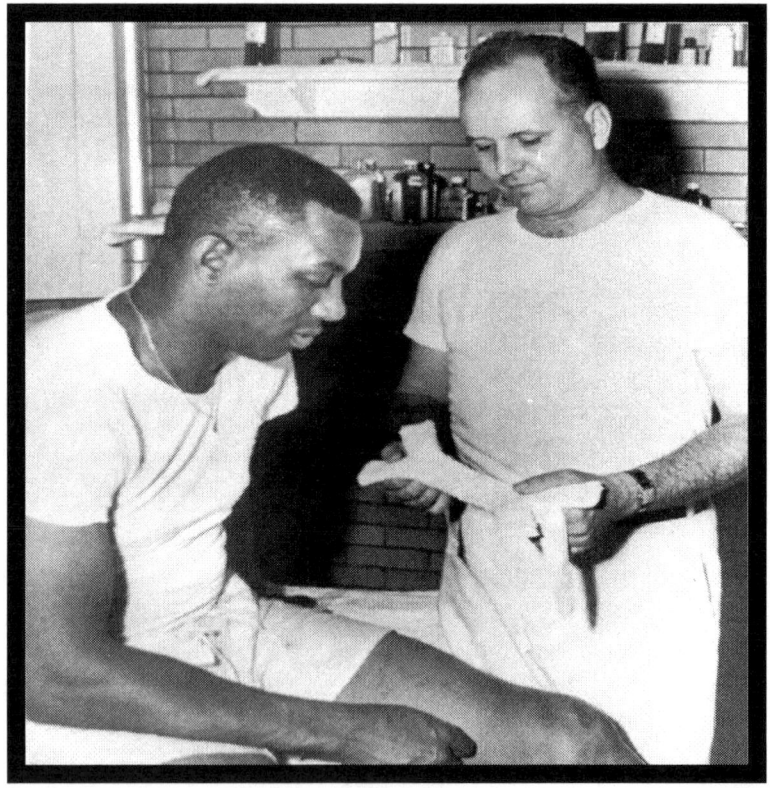

*Easter with Indians team trainer Wally Bock, who had the unenviable task of dealing with a myriad of Easter injuries. (Cleveland Indians team archives)*

The Indians looked poised to make a pennant run in 1950, featuring a new-look offense and anchored by a starting rotation that starred three future Hall of Famers (Bob Feller, Early Wynn, and Bob Lemon). For the first time since the conclusion of World War II, Feller would not be named the Opening Day starting pitcher for the Indians. Player/Manager Lou Boudreau opted instead for Lemon after a strong spring showing (and an equally weak spring for Feller). Holding down the catching duties was veteran Jim Hegan, who had been with the club since signing as an amateur before the 1938 season. Vernon would man first base, Joe Gordon and Boudreau would cover the middle infield at second base and shortstop, respectively. New to the fold was rookie third baseman Al 'Flip' Rosen, with the club having released popular and long-tenured third baseman Ken Keltner. Given his Jewish faith, Rosen also known as the "Hebrew Hammer".

Like Easter, Rosen spent a fair amount of time in 1949 with the Padres, where he notched a .319 batting average, slugging 14 home runs in 83 games. Unlike Easter, who tended to (at least publicly) take racial barbs and prejudice somewhat even-keeled, Rosen did not. Rosen had a terrible temper and would often try to enter the stands to challenge fans who threw anti-Semitic remarks his way. Being a former prizefighter, it was certainly a good thing for the bigoted fans he had teammates like Easter to hold him back.[14]

Rosen, once told by a Chicago Cubs scout to "get a lunch pail and go home," at an open tryout, was looking to make good with the Indians his first full season as a big leaguer.[15]

Despite their obvious personality differences, Easter adored Flip. There were few in the clubhouse whom Easter trusted more. They both had a strong sense of trying to be professional in a climate that was not particularly conducive to them due to prejudice. They rooted for each other's success. One time, Rosen had hit a walk-off, game-winning home run. Everyone quickly ran out of the Indians dugout to greet him at home plate to celebrate. A notable absentee to the celebration was Easter, who hadn't made it out of the dugout. Upon further inspection, Easter was so excited for Rosen that he jumped so far out of his seat when the ball left the yard, that he knocked himself out on the cement dugout ceiling. Imagine his teammates surprise when they returned to the dugout to find Easter unconscious on the ground.[16]

In the outfield, Veteran Dale Mitchell would cover left field, the 26-year old Larry Doby in center field. Easter, making his first Opening Day roster, had earned the starting nod in right field. They were slated to take on the Detroit Tigers.[17]

Local journalist Howard Babcock set the scene for Opening Day:

> "This is the day that thousands of Clevelanders take sick at their jobs and just happen to stroll into Lakefront stadium, thinking it's a doctor's office. Or perhaps a sudden death in the family or a dental appointment will require Cleveland's baseball bugs to take leave from their places of employment and scamper down to the stadium at 3:00pm...As has been the custom for many years, the mayor – Thomas A. Burke – will toss the first ball, probably a wild pitch, and then will be relieved by right-hander Bob Lemon, the Tribe's ace who won 22 games last season."[18]

It may have taken 12 plate appearances before his first hit the previous season, but when hitting in the bottom of the first inning, Easter rocketed a single straight back at pitcher Fred Hutchinson, "Large Luscious Easter almost put Hutch on a crutch with a first-inning screamliner that went between the Detroit pitcher's knees like a bat out of the bad place," James E. Doyle of the *Plain Dealer* reported.[19] He would fly out three more times to end the game, a 7-6 extra inning defeat for the home team. Doby and Rosen both homered in the loss.

Easter collected a hit each of the season's first five games, including a double, along with four walks. After the first two games of the season were played at home, the next 13 were road games. In early May, the Indians visited Boston to take on the Red Sox for a three game set. Easter started the final two, going hitless in six at-bats. As the *Plain Dealer* alluded to on May 5, there may have been more than just typical 'bench jockeying' between Easter and the Red Sox bench. "Fortunately, Luke Easter is a good-natured guy who can take a lot of 'riding', for that's precisely what he got from the Boston Red Sox dugout here yesterday and today." The write-up continued, "It's a good thing Luke can keep his temper," an unnamed teammate said, "I don't know what I'd do if I had to take what he did."[20] Such was commonplace for many of the black players in the league, particularly when they would visit teams and cities who weren't integrated, such as Boston (who wouldn't integrate until 1959, being the last team to do so).

After the Boston series, Easter and the Indians went to New York to play the Yankees next for a quick, day-night doubleheader on May 6. Easter was carrying a .192 batting average with one RBI through eight games.[21]

Facing eventual 16-game winner Allie Reynolds, himself a former Indian traded to the Yankees in exchange for Joe Gordon, Easter dug into the batter's box in the top of the third inning of the first game. With Hegan standing on second and Vernon on first, he unleashed on a Reynolds serving, "sending a bazooka blast that hit the facing of the second deck."[22] Easter's first career home run was a big one, giving the Indians a 3-0 lead over the rival Yankees. Two innings later, and again off Reynolds, Easter scorched a liner down the right field line, and would score on an ensuing Doby single. The Indians would hold on to win 5-4.

The second game of the set began immediately after the first contest was settled. Fred Sanford was on the mound to start for the Bombers in the second game. In the first inning, and again with Vernon standing on-base, Easter picked right up where he left off, planting a Sanford offering in the right field seats for a quick 2-0 first inning lead, his second home run of the day. Though the Indians would lose the second game 7-4, Easter's efforts for the day did not go unnoticed. "Luke Easter, a big flop until now, hammered two homers, accounting for five runs," The *Plain Dealer* reported. All told, Easter went three-for-six with two home runs and five runs batted in on the day. It easily represented his finest day as a professional, and his average jumped to .250 on the season.[23]

Two days after the New York series, Easter was finally given the first base job in a shakeup of the infield. The Indians were in fifth place with a 6-8 record, and Boudreau thought change was in order. Benched was Vernon (.145 batting average) and Joe Gordon (.146). Johnny Berardino would hold down the second sack. Allie Clark would be penciled in to play right field.[24]

By the end of May, the Indians were struggling (20-17, third place, seven games back), and Easter was (again) struggling to find consistency at the plate. "His hits come about as often as Halle's Comet," lamented *The Daily Times* out of New Philadelphia, Ohio.[25] Entering June, Easter was hitting .230, with only three home runs and 11 RBI. Though Vernon had been benched due to ineffective play, Boudreau was offered little choice, playing both men until one started streaking. Boudreau had allegedly gone as far as saying Easter had "flunked" his trial as a major leaguer.[26]

*The Sporting News* called Luke Easter "the most booed player in the history of Cleveland Stadium."[27] An Ohio advertisement for a used 1947 Chevy Club Coupe was even pouring it on, stating in the description that "Luke Easter's club may be no good. But this one bats 1.000."[28] One might suppose a silver lining for Easter at this point was that he did not read the paper during the season, at least not the sports pages anyway. Easter's wife Vergil "keeps a scrap book and he reads all about himself after he puts his glove up for the winter,"[29] the *Wilmington Daily Press Journal* in California reported.

One fiercely loyal faction of fans still backed Easter, as historian Daniel J. Cattau notes, "If adult fans were divided about Easter, children seldom were. Nothing kept Easter from talking to kids. He regularly dropped by sandlot games unannounced, dispensing tips and encouragement." Luke was once asked when he would retire. Curtly, he insisted when the kids quit on him, he would quit too.[30]

Easter, insistent he would break out of the slump, the worst of his career, saw the calendar flip from May to June. With it, his fortunes as well. Easter, better-prepared for the racial taunts and jeers from the Boston dugout and crowd, clubbed home runs in the first two contests of the month, both in Boston. Between June

3 and June 18, Easter would notch seven multi-hit games. Between June 22 and 23, Easter hit four round trippers, including the longest one in Cleveland Municipal Stadium history (the 'Prodigious Swat').

Easter ended the month having played in 29 games, recorded 39 hits, including five doubles, a triple, 11 home runs and 31 runs batted in. His batting average for the month was .331. With the 15 walks he drew, his on-base percentage swelled to a .406 mark.[31]

For once, the hometown crowd wasn't booing the giant rookie. At least, most of the crowd, anyway.

"Isn't it curious how quickly a fellow can get into public favor after being confined to the doghouse?" *The Salem News* out of Salem, Ohio asked. "We're referring to the sudden emergency of Lucious 'Luke' Easter from a target for boos to a position of at least half-hearted tolerance by the Cleveland fans. We saw big Luke come up to the plate in the first inning of Friday's game and he was greeted by a torrent of inverted cheers (boos) from the majority of the crowd." In recapping a home run trot, the musings read "As he rounded the sacks he was accorded the first Cleveland cheers he's heard all season. Unlike Ted Williams, he tipped his cap to the wolves."[32]

About halfway through Easter's excellent month, June 14, Greenberg was finally able to find a suitor for the services of Mickey Vernon. About 18 months after the initial trade that sent Vernon and pitcher Early Wynn to the Indians from the Washington Senators (mostly for first baseman Eddie Robinson), the Indians sent him back to Washington, this time in exchange for pitcher Dick Weik.[33]

Most importantly, the Indians were surging in the standings, having gone 19-10 in June and 20-11 in July. At 59-38, they stood just two games back from the first place Yankees. By July's end, Easter continued to rake, having belted 21 home runs and driving in 60 runs.[34]

In early August, *Collier's* published a feature story about Easter titled, 'They're Gonna Like Big Luke'. The piece, written by managing editor Gordon Manning, chronicles Easter's meteoric rise while highlighting his previous four seasons with the Crescents, Grays, Padres, and Indians. Manning painted a scene he observed as sportswriters were watching Easter take batting practice before a game:

> "A veteran sports scribe standing behind the cage with Manager Lou Boudreau and a group of other writers whistled expressively. 'There's the only player I've ever seen in the big leagues,' he said, 'who can make the pitcher duck on a home-run ball.'
>
> 'Yeah,' added another press box tenant, 'that ball could kill a man when it goes through the box that way.'"[35]

Manning also recalls an instance in 1949 when Red Sox second baseman Bobby Doerr fielded a blistering ground ball from the bat of Easter, "The force of the blow spun Doerr around like a top. When Bobby finally recovered the ball he had knocked down, Easter was on first base."[36]

For the first time, at least nationally, the story also shed some light on the humble beginnings of Easter. Interestingly enough, there was nary a word regarding his Mississippi Delta origins. Interesting, though not surprising. "Luke never did want anyone to know he was from Mississippi," his brother J.C. later recalled, 'People would tease you if they knew you were from Mississippi. I guess Luke wanted to avoid that."[37] Manning briefly broaches the topic of Easter's actual age, starting "If he's fudging his age, though, it's not an uncommon trick in the big leagues where everyone tries to stay young forever."[38]

At the end of the 1950 season, sharp divide separated the top four from the bottom four teams in the American League. The top four teams won at least 92 games, the other four won 67 games or fewer. After the final games of the season were finished on October 1, the Indians record stood at 92-62. This signaled a three-game improvement over the previous season. Unfortunately for the Indians, in the standings they were looking up at the

Yankees (98 wins), the Tigers (95), and the Red Sox (94). 25 games separated the fourth place Indians from the fifth place Washington Senators, who won 67 games. The White Sox (60 wins), Browns (58), and Athletics (52) rounded out the American League.[39] There had rarely been such a disparity between the two halves of any league.

Down the stretch, the closest the Indians would be to the league's top spot was on September 7. Sporting an 80-54 record, the Indians were four games behind the Yankees. Though they would notch a 12-8 record after that, it was not nearly enough in a competitive American League. The Yankees went on to sweep the Philadelphia Phillies in the World Series.[40]

Over in the National League, Easter's old teammate and friend Sam 'The Jet' Jethroe won the Rookie of the Year award. Jethroe hit .273, while slugging 28 doubles and 18 home runs for the Boston Braves. His 35 steals led both leagues.

Easter would finish the 1950 season having played in 141 of the club's 154 games. He would finish the season with 28 home runs and 107 RBI, both second to fellow rookie Rosen's marks of 37 and 116 respectively. His average sat at .280, with a swollen on-base percentage of .373 courtesy of 70 walks. Easter was also hit by ten pitches, the highest mark in all of baseball (ironically, tied for first with teammate Al Rosen).

Of all the ballplayers age 34-and-over in baseball, only Joe DiMaggio had a finer season than Easter, with 32 home runs, 122 RBI. Though it didn't translate to a higher place in the standing, thanks to rookies Easter and Rosen the Indians would score 131 more runs (a 16% increase) and hit 52 more home runs (32%) in 1950 over the previous, offensively-challenged 1949 season.[41]

As was Easter modus operandi, he would barnstorm for a fair amount of the offseason once again in 1950. Starting less than two weeks after the regular season was over, he struck up a band of black 'All-Stars' to hit the road.

The 1950 squad was headlined by New York Giants Monte Irvin and Hank Thompson, as well as third baseman Ray Dandridge.

Dandridge had just been named the Most Valuable Player in the American Association, a Triple-A league, as was a former Newark Eagle.[42]

The tour started with three contests in Virginia against Danny Litwhiler's (of the Cincinnati Reds) 'National League All-Stars' on October 10. Litwhiler's team was headlined by Dodger Carl Furillo, Phillie Del Ennis, and former Indian Mickey Vernon.[43] Easter's squad would defeat Litwhiler's in a clean sweep, 4-3, 5-4 and 5-3.[44,45]

Most of the next two weeks were spent in Alabama, Mississippi, and Texas, where Easter's All-Stars mostly competed with the Birmingham Black Barons and the Negro American League All-Stars. On October 22, Easter was involved in a collision at the plate, which forced him to miss a couple games after receiving four stitches above his right eye.[46] The tour would end in Tampa, Florida, on November 6, marking Easter's first appearance in the city.[47]

November would prove to be an interesting month for Easter and the Indians. On the tenth, it was announced that longtime player/manager Lou Boudreau would not be retained heading into the 1951 campaign, opting for former big league catcher and Indianapolis Indians manager Al Lopez.

"It is our feeling that Cleveland fans want a winning team above anything else," team owner Ellis Ryan stated, "and in our opinion Al Lopez, who has compiled an almost unbelievable record, is the man to likely produce one."[48]

Boudreau commented from his Illinois home "I'm terribly sorry to leave Cleveland – please tell that to the fans. They were wonderful to me."[49]

After 13 seasons (nine as player/manager), the seven-time All-Star, one-time American League Most Valuable Player, the captain of the 1948 World Series-winning team, the 'Boy Manager' Lou Boudreau's tenure in Cleveland was finished. 'The Good Kid' Boudreau had won 728 games as manager.

On November 18, there was a rumor swirling that Greenberg was open to trading Easter, and that the lowly Chicago White Sox in exchange for former Indians first baseman Eddie Robinson and 15-game winner Bill Wight. It was the White Sox general manager Frank 'Trader' Lane (who would have a controversial tenure in the same position with the Indians later in the decade) who came out and denied such reports. "I'm not interested in the trade," Lane stated, "I'm not ready to have White Sox fans escort me to the city limits with demands of 'be on your way'."[50]

Luke Easter was to remain in Cleveland for the 1951 season. With that in mind, he took perhaps his most cushy offseason job yet; he hit the road with Abe Saperstein and his Harlem Globetrotters, serving them in the capacity of traveling secretary and "official greeter" until he was to report for spring training.[51]

Hot off an impressive rookie campaign, and enjoying his celebrity with the ever-popular Globetrotters, it was good to be Luke Easter.

# 9.

# Different Year, Still Chasin' the Yankees

*"Easter gives you the willies. When he walks up there with that bat you get the feeling you're pitching uphill."*[1]

*-Ed Lopat, New York Yankees pitcher, whom Easter hit at a .417 clip during the 1951 season.*

Heading into the 1951 season, the 35-year old (29-year old according to the media guide) Luke Easter took advantage of a new rule in baseball that allowed players to report to spring training camp up to two weeks early. Perhaps hearing about Easter's side job during the offseason, Hank Greenberg pushed him to arrive early with the rookies. "The only regular I've invited to start February 15 is Easter," he said. "I want to make sure he's in good physical shape."[2]

If Greenberg had any trepidation about Easter enjoying a little too much limelight during the offseason, he may have been correct. However, if he was worried Easter wouldn't show up to camp in shape, his fears would have been alleviated when, arriving with pitcher Sam Zoldak, Easter came into camp weighing 234 pounds. He told reporters he hoped to shave two pounds off and play at 232. "I took pretty good care of myself over the winter. I hope to have a real good year, and if I do, I think we can win the pennant," Easter proclaimed shortly after reporting.[3]

The Indians expectations were lofty heading into the campaign, particularly due to the previous season's fourth-place showing. There was excitement with another full season to showcase the new-look offense. Easter was going to be counted on to provide more power and run production, and a bulk of the Indians offense attack was just 27 years of age, including Al Rosen, Ray

Boone, Bobby Avila, and Larry Doby. Jim Hegan and Dale Mitchell would provide an additional veteran presence.

Offense aside, the starting rotation was where season-long success hinged. The Indians could boast of starting pitching that had been dubbed 'The Big Four'. Returning to the fray was Bob Feller, Mike Garcia, Early Wynn, and Bob Lemon. The four combined for 68 victories the season before.

Greenberg, ever-competitive, himself had flatly predicted a pennant for the Indians in 1950. Though the revelation that had not come to fruition, it was all but certain he had high hopes for the 1951 edition of the Indians.[4]

Though Easter and several other Indians regulars had arrived a couple weeks before, the entire squad was present for spring training by March 5. Al Lopez, the new manager, took a couple days to take stock in his hitters, and quickly announced that Easter would bat third in the lineup heading into the 1951 campaign. "From what I've seen so far," Lopez told reporters, "I believe Easter will be our greatest home run threat this year. A club's best left-handed hitter should bat third because he gets to the player more often and is less likely to hit into a double play and spoil a rally."[5]

On March 7, Easter injured his elbow in yet another spring training collision. "Luke Easter's elbow is Cleveland's Achilles heel,' Al Wolf wrote the *Los Angeles Times*. "That vulnerable heel, you may recall, proved slightly fatal to the mythological hero. This elbow could similarly affect the Indians' hopped-up pennant hopes."[6]

After sitting out for nearly three weeks after his latest in a bizarre string of spring training injuries, Easter returned to action on March 27. Fortunately, there didn't seem to be any lingering issues with Easter's elbow; in his first exhibition game back, he hit three singles in a 17-7 rout of the St. Louis Browns.[7]

The Indians would sport a new-look infield than the previous season. Gone were Boudreau and Joe Gordon, in were second baseman Bobby Avila from Mexico (one of the few Latino players in the league), and shortstop Ray Boone, who had been with the organization since 1942. Easter and Rosen would once again bookend the infield, playing the corner spots.

Also new in camp was outfielder Harry Simpson, a 25-year old veteran of the Negro Leagues, where he played for the Philadelphia Stars. In two short seasons in the minors, Simpson had already tallied 64 homes runs. Much like Easter, he tore the cover off the Pacific Coast League baseballs as well, hitting 33 home runs and driving in 156 the previous season in San Diego.[8] He had acquired the nickname of 'Suitcase' on account of his size 13 shoes, likening him to a popular cartoon character of the day with comically large feet.[9]

Not one to be short on confidence, when Hank Greenberg had visited him the previous October in San Diego, Greenberg was still buzzing about the season that Easter had put together in 1950.

"I know a player who can hit better than Easter," Simpson slyly asserted.

"Who?" asked Greenberg.

"Me." Simpson self-assuredly answered.[10]

Greenberg returned to Cleveland rooting for 'Suitcase' the following season.

Having just finally recovered from the chipped elbow less than two weeks before, injury struck unlucky Easter again. And again on the eve of the start of the season. On April 8, during an exhibition with the New York Giants, Easter did a "perfect but disastrous split" while digging out an errant throw at first base. "He suffered a severely torn muscle in his left thigh and is almost certain to miss the American League opener with the Detroit Tigers,"[11] the *Akron Beacon Journal* wrote, complete with a photograph of Easter's calamitous splits.

Even up to as far as Opening Day morning, Easter's status remained uncertain whether he would be able to play, with many papers penciling in Minnie Minoso as the temporary first baseman. Despite another hard-luck spring regarding injuries,

Easter was inserted into the Opening Day lineup, batting third and playing first base.

In addition to the infield, the rest of the projected Opening Day starters heading into 1951 was Jim Hegan would once again be behind the plate as catcher. The outfield would look similar, as Doby would be in center field, Dale Mitchell in left field, and Bob Kennedy in right field. Kennedy was the Opening Day starter in that position in 1949 as well before making way for the debut of Easter. For the second consecutive season, Bob Lemon would get the ball to start the first game.[12]

Simpson and Minoso would also both make the big league team, making the Cleveland Indians the first Major League team with four black players on the roster.

Against future Hall-of-Famer Hal Newhouser, Easter would drive in Avila in the first inning for the first run of the season, en route to a 2-1 victory over the Tigers. Easter, one of the players claimed, "Was the best one-legged hitters in baseball," after a two-for-three, one RBI performance.[13]

Through the first eight games of the season, the Indians were 7-1. Easter, bum leg and all, was hitting .423. Though he hadn't hit any home runs, he had already drove in six runs and taken five walks.

But Easter couldn't catch a break. On April 28, during just the eighth game of the season, a rout of the Browns, Easter snapped a tendon in his left knee and would miss a couple weeks of action. "What have I done wrong?" Easter wondered aloud from the trainer's table after the game. Local writer Jim Schlemmer surmised that both leg injuries could have been the result of a lack of conditioning Easter was able to do while nursing his chipped elbow, "And forcing him back into the lineup before he was actually ready to return." He also penned that players on the Indians bench reported they could hear his tendon snap as reached for the throw from Avila during the game.[14]

While Easter was sidelined, Greenberg executed what would be considered one of the poorest moves of his executive career. On April 30, a three-team trade sent Minoso packing his bags for the

Chicago White Sox. Reporters openly questioned whether the Indians had a quota of three black players that year, and with Easter, Doby, Minoso, and Simpson meaning one had to go. Greenberg himself, rather prophetically claimed that Minoso would become "One of the really good players of our time."[15] Much to Greenberg's chagrin, Minoso would be selected for five of the next seven All-Star games as a member of the White Sox, hitting .326 while leading the league in triples and stolen bases in 1951.[16]

With Easter out of the lineup, the Indians swooned, and were a fifth place team when he returned to the lineup on May 18. Though Easter would crack four hits in his first eight at-bats back, the Indians continued to falter, falling to 12-14 on the season and a sixth place standing.[17]

By the beginning of July, the team's fortunes had slightly reversed as they sported a 37-30 record, but were still in fourth place in the American League. That day, fans were treated to a vintage Bob Feller performance, as the 32-year old hurler spun up his third (and final) career no-hitter, as the Indians beat the Tigers 2-1 on July 1. Easter knocked in both runs, including a clutch single in the bottom of the eighth inning which proved to be the difference to back Feller's gem.[18]

Two days before Easter's 36th birthday on August 2, the second place Indians beat the Washington Senators 5-2 to push their record to 60-39. They would proceed to win their next 12 consecutive games. The 13-game winning streak was the team's longest since 1942, when that club (during then-24-year old Lou Boudreau's first season as manager) also won 13 games. The club emerged from the streak in first place, up by 2.5 games over the rival Yankees.

Interestingly enough, while the team was hot as a firecracker, Easter was cold as a postgame clubhouse shower; during the 13 game span, he hit below .150 with only one extra base hit and three runs batted in. It would be revealed later that much of Easter's hitting woes during this time was again because of his knee, which had "swelled up like a balloon" according to the local papers.¹⁹ He would miss a few games.

Greenberg's pennant prophecy, albeit a year tardy, was looking more and more probable. Between August 8 and September 16, the club spent nearly every single day in first place. On the 16th, the team was 90-55 and tied for first in the league. Fortunately for the Indians, they were primed to distance themselves from the Yankees, as five of their final nine games were against the Detroit Tigers. To that point, the Indians had won 16 of the season's 17 contests against the Tigers. Inversely, the Yankees faced the always-tough Boston Red Sox in eight of their final nine games.²⁰

Bob Feller (middle), between the offensive heroes of his third career no-hitter. Sam Chapman (left) tripled and scored a run, while Easter drove both runs home in the 2-1 win. (Cleveland Indians team archives)

As fate would have it, the Indians would lose four of five to the Tigers, a team they had utterly dominated for the first five months of the season. The lone win was on the penultimate game of the season. Easter hit two home runs (his 26th and 27th on the season), and drove in five (pushing his total to 103) to power the club to a 7-6 victory. The Yankees would win seven of their last nine to make a successful, and blistering, pennant push, leaving the Indians in a distant second place. Despite having been tied for the league lead 10 days earlier, the Indians floundered and finished five games behind the Yankees. As they had the previous two seasons, the Yankees would go on to win the World Series.

During a World Series interview, Greenberg applauded Al Rosen's work at the plate and at third base. The local press didn't take kindly to the compliment. "And that we nominate as the joke of the year," wrote Loren Tibbals of the *Akron Beacon Journal* in an article titled "Who Are the Indians Kidding?". After hearing that Lopez also commended the infield, he continued "For my money, the Clevelanders could offer for grabs all of the infielders except Roberto Avila at second. Or in other words, they can send Luke Easter, Al Rosen and Ray Boone any place except back to their 1951 stations." Tibbals finished the piece writing "The Indians didn't convince me they were dead serious about the 1951 junior league scramble – and after hearing from Lopez and Greenberg, here's one guy who's not convinced they're serious about '52 either."[21]

The backlash from the fans and many of the pundits in Cleveland as a result of the lackluster stretch run continued all offseason.

Though dejected as a result of the late season collapse, there was still plenty of optimism in the Indians camp. Aside from a couple exceptions, the Indians had finished in second with much of the same personnel that had finished fourth the season before. Owner Ellis Ryan, pleased with Greenberg's work, rewarded him with a two-year contract (which would later be amended to three years). The move drew the ire of the Cleveland fans. The *Plain Dealer's* Gordon Cobbledick sang Greenberg's praises that offseason as well:

> "Greenberg has done exactly what Ryan has said he has done – an excellent job. No swivel-chaired stuffed shirt, High Henry works harder at his job than any other man in baseball except the one

who invented hard work, Bill Veeck. It'll pay off. Just wait and see."[22]

For his part, Easter finished the season with a .270 average, swatting 27 home runs and driving in 103 runs. Though the marks were a few ticks off his previous season, he missed a total of 26 games, mostly due to injury. As an indication of his value, the team's was 82-46 with Easter playing (.646 winning percentage), 11-15 when he didn't (.423).

He played nearly the entire season with his left knee still aching him daily. It was announced in mid-October that he would have another procedure on his knee on November 13.[23] He would first complete a barnstorming tour with the Negro All-Stars, managed by none other than Jackie Robinson and featured Easter, Doby, and Sam Jethroe among others. Naturally, he hit .400 on the circuit even with the hobbled knee.[24]

A few days before the procedure was slated, he met with Greenberg for lunch in Cleveland. The two always seem to maintain a friendly, if not high-spirited relationship.

"What we need," Greenberg said facetiously, "is a first baseman. A solid first baseman – not one made of putty." A statement which drew a grin out of Easter.

"Poor fella had to play the season on one leg and still he drove in 103 runs," Easter fired back, lapsing into the third person, "I think he did pretty good. How many do you suppose he'd driven in if he had two good legs?"

Easter proceeded to share his offseason conditioning plans with Greenberg, and how he intended to strengthen his bad knee.

In speaking about the pending operation, Easter told Greenberg that "No matter how it turns out, my knee can't feel any worse than it did last season."

"So, with two good legs you should drive in 200 runs." Greenberg lightheartedly concluded.[25]

The surgery, performed at Johns Hopkins was deemed a success. Three weeks later he was off his crutches and walking among the Cleveland snowdrifts. "The man said walk," Luke said referring to the doctor's orders, "So I did."[26]

Heading into spring training for 1952, the veteran Easter was entering into his third full season. Though he led the team in both home runs and runs batted in the year before, much of the general public still considered the showing to be lackluster. As it were, it was always difficult for Easter to capture a majority of positive public sentiment, regardless of his performance. It was an unfortunate hallmark of his time in The Forest City.

Physically, he was far from peak shape. Despite his best efforts at rehabilitation, his knees ached daily, he was suffering from chronic headaches, thanks to a degenerative eye condition.

While both organizational and personal expectations as high as ever, Easter was very privately dealing with the physical signs of his actual age. The wear and tear on his body was becoming a personal concern. How would he perform with everyone expecting 'Big Luke' to be at his best for the 1952 season?

## 10.

## Well, I'll be Damned.

*"His comeback is the most amazing thing I have ever seen."*[1]

-Hank Greenberg, Cleveland Indians general manager

Arriving at Tucson for spring training in 1952 netted a pleasant surprise. The Santa Rita Hotel, where the team had lodged for years in the spring, had dropped their policy of barring blacks from staying there. Since 1948, the black players on the Indians were relegated to the home of Chester and Lucille Willis, and away from the rest of the team.[2] This was a particularly important year for this sign of progress; of the nine black baseball players who would see action in the American League that season, six would suit up for the Indians, including Easter, Larry Doby, Harry 'Suitcase' Simpson, Dave Pope, Quincy Trouppe, and pitcher 'Toothpick Sam' Jones.

To help jumpstart the club's offensive, Greenberg concocted a plan to have a 'batting school' take place in mid-February before formal spring training began. The instructors were Greenberg himself, Indian legend Tris Speaker, and manager Al Lopez. The pupils? The heart of the batting order, including Easter, Doby, Ray Boone, Jim Hegan and 'Suitcase' Simpson. If their collective batting average wasn't raised 20 points from the season before, Greenberg would donate $1,000 to charity.[3]

Much to player's surprise (and vexation), there was far less traditional batting practice attached to the syllabus of the batting school, but much more work with Greenberg at a chalkboard and poring over multiple seasons worth of matchup data. "Any good hitter I ever knew used a bat to hit with. He didn't get his hits with a piece of chalk and a blackboard," Luke playfully grumbled. Doby would ultimately flat-out refuse to attend, given his contract dispute with Greenberg (who was attempted to cut his salary by a quarter).[4]

The idea, though innovative, did not prove to be successful during spring training. The vaunted infield sported a poorly .222 collective batting average with less than a week left of the spring. Avila was hitting .260, Easter .235, Al Rosen .233, and Ray Boone .212. Despite the swoon by the starters, Greenberg and Lopez didn't have many options; the backup infielders were hitting .154.[5] Easter's batting average was crippled by a stretch where he hadn't hit safely in 16 consecutive at-bats.[6] The pain in his left knee was still considerable, having fluid removed from it just before the beginning of spring training.

"Rosen and Easter are running quite a race for looking weakest at bat," Jim Schlemmer of the *Akron Beacon Journal* wrote, "Easter hasn't a hit since last Saturday at Dallas. He has gone completely off his timing." Easter, ever-sly and sporting at least a façade of confidence, grinned and responded that it rather unusual to have two good legs under him, and maybe he'd have to learn how to hit all over again.[7]

In an interview the following day, again with Schlemmer, he stated that he anticipated he was good for four or five more seasons, promising to retire at 35 (Easter, of course, was already 36). Overhearing the remark, pitcher Lou Brissie playfully interjected, "Luke, if you're quitting at 35, this must be your last season," Easter allegedly gave him an appropriate retort in response.[8]

The Indians penned by many pundits across the country to make a run at the pennant again in 1952, stumbled into the regular season on an offensive slump.

Unfortunately, at least for Easter, his slump persisted. By the end of April, Easter was hitting a measly .173, by the end of May, a paltry .191, or "about 50 points below his playing weight" one local writer wrote.[9] Though he had still showed some of his trademark power, clubbing seven home runs. Halfway through May, Easter was put on ice for several games while the swelling in his knees subsided.

Fortunately for the Indians, despite Easter's struggles, the club stood in first place at the end of May with a 25-17 record. Per tradition, the galvanized Cleveland faithful, whether fan or sportswriter, jumped at the opportunity to criticize their often-beleaguered first baseman. Only this time, the rising tide looked like it was going to sink the boat.

In responding to a June 4 letter from a reader, Al Bricker, sports editor at *The Daily Times* out of New Philadelphia, Ohio, concluded after thanking the reader for the letter (with anti-Easter sentiments within), "Luke does have a lot of fans who think his 'long ball' is one thing that is holding the Indians up as high as they are. We ran into an Easter fan just the other day, or last week, or maybe it was last year – at least we heard there was an Easter fan!"[10]

The call to bench Easter continued to increase in volume despite a slight bump in his average and production in the early going of June. "Members of the anti-Easter faction do not include just fans, but investors in the club as well," the *Plain Dealer* reported, "Some stockholders, prematurely panic-stricken, would have Ellis Ryan option Luke to Siberia and not on a 24-hour recall."[11]

Every time Easter walked up to the plate at Cleveland Municipal Stadium, the booing from the home crowd were almost deafening.

Publicly, Easter was stoic regarding the reception he had received for most of his career. "I hear the boos. You can't turn them off. But I'm not losing any sleep over them...I'd rather have them boo me than the other players on our club. I've got broad shoulders."[12]

Behind the scenes, Greenberg was already trying to rid the club of Easter. On June 6, it was reported that he was in talks with the Philadelphia Athletics and their first baseman, former Easter barnstorming mate Ferris Fain.[13] Greenberg, a constant defender of Easter since he was called up almost three years earlier, was at the end of his rope. The constant grumbling from upper management and the press, the constant boos from the home crowds, the fact that Easter was always trying to push his body to the maximum while injured had Greenberg thinking of Easter's best interests. Greenberg really enjoyed Easter, but thought maybe a change in scenery could help revitalize his career.

On the same day of the trade talks, the ever-pragmatic *Plain Dealer* sports editor Gordon Cobbledick came to the aid of Easter. "This isn't the first time the Cleveland rooters have hollered for Easter's thinly-carpeted scalp, and yet the big guy is one of the two American leaguers who have batted in more than 100 runs in each of the last two seasons."[14]

Bob Dixon from *The Evening Independent* out of Massillon, Ohio was another one of the few to back Easter, "We've heard the criticism that 'Luke hasn't been trying,' but you can write that off as so much baloney. He is one of the hardest working players on the club, but because of his size he...may always give the appearance of an easy-going player."[15]

On June 16, having been put through the ringer by the fans, local press, and having spent time on the trade block, manager Al Lopez decided it best to bench Easter.

"'Boo Birds' Harangue Luke: Easter Benched Because Of Fans" read the *Akron Beacon Journal* the following day. Lopez was quoted saying:

> "The fans have been on Luke hot and heavy since we came home and even before we went East. Luke has been giving us the best he has and I didn't want him to have to take the booing and suffer the humiliation this crowd would heap upon him."[16]

At the end of June, despite being third in the Major Leagues in home runs (11, trailing only Gil Hodges and Walt Dropo), and receiving 300,000 All-Star game votes, Easter was demoted to the triple-A Indianapolis Indians of the American Association. His shattered confidence, as well as his paltry .208 batting average was undoubtedly the culprit.

"If Luke has not regained his batting at the end of three weeks, then he never will," Lopez told the press. Easter, self-confidence undoubtedly shaken stated 'If this will help me get my hittin' right again, then it'll help the team and I'm all for it. I'm looking forward to being back real soon."[17]

Dave Pope, a 27-year old black outfielder who had been playing in Indianapolis, was selected to take Easter's roster spot. The Indians of Cleveland were 37-32 at the time of his demotion.[18]

Easter, having just received news of his demotion from Greenberg himself, went into the clubhouse to clean out his locker. For the 36-year old first baseman not even hitting his weight, there was no guarantee he would ever be back as an Indian. The prospects looked bleak, even to the usually supremely self-confident Easter. He had to make haste; he was due in Indianapolis for a game the following day, and it was easily a six-hour drive from Cleveland.

For what he perceived to be possibly the final time, he went through his fan mail, delivered directly to his locker. After a couple years of receiving such mail, it had all began to look the same. On that particular day, one letter stuck out. The note implored Luke to 'keep your head up through the tough times' and 'keep plugging away'. The note was signed by Willoughby Township eight-year old Daniel Jack, who had clearly been reading the local rags and felt his hero needed encouragement. Easter send Jack an autograph and a note of thanks, and tucked the child's note inside his billfold as he accepted his role with the minor league Indianapolis Indians. Of all the fan mail he had ever received, the note was a one of the few pieces he decided to keep.[19]

The Indianapolis Indians weren't overly thrilled to welcome Easter into the fold; one unnamed player didn't mince words. "We're losing a center fielder (Pope), of which we have none now, and we are getting a first baseman of which we have two already." Others pointed out that the Indians were "robbed" of a proven triple-A player only to be saddled with a washed out first baseman "Who's fielding had been as unsteady as his knee."[20]

Welcomed or not, Easter made his way to Indianapolis and quickly made a splash, slamming a 385-foot home run and laying a flawless first base in his first game on June 3rd.[21]

The following day, he notched four hits in six at-bats, including yet another round tripper. Through six games, Easter was hitting .454 (10-22) with four home runs.[22] In an almost miraculous string of 14 games, Easter hit .340 rapped out 17 hits, including six home runs, 12 runs batted in, and ten walks.[23]

Through the demotion, the big slugger had finally found his hitting rhythm once again.

Within days of Luke's absence, and hearing of his successes in Indianapolis, his backers were clamoring to have him back. In a stroke of bad luck, Pope crashed into an outfield wall during his debut[24], and it was becoming more and more evident that the right fielder Simpson was not a natural first baseman.[25]

"'How're you gonna keep him down on the farm?' howl Luke Easter rooters in Cleveland, gladdened by the big guy's slugging for Indianapolis,"[26] wrote the *Plain Dealer*. Another spirited fan penned a little ditty for the occasion, titled 'Can't Hold Him Down?'

> "Luke Easter, that ol' swattin'man,
> Just won't be a forgotten man."[27]

After just 14 spectacular games in the Hoosier State, Easter was recalled to the Indians on July 14, to be ready for the next day's tilt against the New York Yankees.[28] Easter's confidence was back, and he believed he owed at least a bit of that to the letter of encouragement he received from the small boy while on his way out of Cleveland. He would keep it in his billfold the rest of the season.[29]

Before the start of the game, and having just joined the team a couple hours earlier, reporters gathered around Easter while he was walking around the diamond. He looked longingly the right field stands at Yankee Stadium. "If I could park one out there tonight," he stated, "I think I'll really get going. That's what I need, I think. A home run in my first day back. Man, how I'd like to lose one tonight."[30]

Easter drew a bases-loaded walk in the first inning against Yankees starter Bob Kuzava. He drew another walk in the third. With the

Indians up 6-0 in the seventh inning, Easter greeted a Joe Ostrowki fastball and sent it in the right field stands for a home run. 'Big Luke's' wish had come true, and he had returned triumphantly in his first game back.[31]

Easter would continue his improbable roll through July, finishing the month with a .345 batting average (raising his average to .224 on the season). Though he only hit three home runs (giving him 14 on the season), his on-base percentage was a whopping .537 courtesy of 15 walks - of which three were intentional. American League pitchers were once again becoming fearful of the big slugger.

After Easter hit a go-ahead three-run home run in 3-2 victory over the Washington Senators on July 27, a fan wrote a tongue-in-cheek letter to Easter, stating "Dear Luke: As a confidence-restorer, that game-winning home run yesterday probably was worth a lot more than two weeks in Indianapolis."[32]

"All I know is that I feel great right now," Easter said at the end of July.[33]

Though he might not have felt great going into August (he didn't start the August 1 game due to stiff knees)[34], he continued to play well. Continuing his implausible, and scorching run, he put together one of the best months of his professional career. Between the first and thirty-first of August, Easter would club nine home runs and drive in a whopping 36 runs, while hitting over .300. The newly-minted 37-year old's career was somehow breathing new life.

Late in the month most of the local papers ran the headline "Easter's Timely Comeback Threatens Yanks' Lead".[35] The Indians, 7.5 games behind the Yankees on July 22, had crept up to just two games back at the end of the month, thanks in no small part to Easter's hitting.

Picking up where he left off in August, Easter would take a three-game hitting streak from August and stretch it into a career-high 16-game hitting streak that ran him through September 13. He clubbed eight home runs during the run and hit .390. "Luke

Easter, former target for Cleveland's 'boo birds' is top man on the hit parade of Indian fans today." Ralph Roden of the Associated Press observed.[36]

At the time of Roden's pronouncement, the Indians only trailed the Yankees by a half game. The Indians finished on a tear, winning 10 of their final 13 games in a desperate sprint for the pennant.

Unfortunately, the only team who was hotter than the Cleveland Indians during that stretch was once again the New York Yankees. They would win 12 of their final 14 games bettering the Indians final record of 93-61 by two games and thus capturing the pennant for the fourth consecutive year.[37]

From the time Easter was called back to the club in mid-July, the 37-year old hit .319 with 20 home runs and 64 runs batted in. The damage was accomplished in a mere 64 games. On the season, Easter hit .263, slugging a career-high 31 home runs, and driving in 97 runs along the way. These numbers were accomplished despite playing in the fewest games since his debut in 1949.[38]

In the span of one season, Luke Easter had not only stooped to the lowliest point of his career, but had also made an almost implausible comeback to success. In doing so, Easter gained what he had been yearning for since came to Cleveland - acceptance from the Cleveland fan base.

Lauding his efforts during the 1952 campaign, *The Sporting News* named Easter their 'Player of the Year'.[39] What a season it had been. Easter had defied odds, and gutted his way to the apex. He had even received 40 points in the Most Valuable Player voting.

Still battling sore knees, Easter decided he would not barnstorm during the offseason for the first time in years. "I'm taking no chances," he told a reporter, "My legs will be ready when the season starts." He had also stated that he lost $6,000 the season before on the barnstorming tour.[40]

In lieu of barnstorming, Easter went into business with his brother-in-law Ray Cash to form 'Ray's Sausage' which operated on the east side of Cleveland (and is still in operation today). In a

*Jet Magazine* feature, Easter revealed that though they only sold 20 pounds of sausage the first week, they were selling 2,300 pounds a day by January of 1953. Each package had a picture of Easter, along with the slogan, "If you want to hit like Luke, eat like Luke!"[41] Ray's Sausage was even slated to be sold at Indians games during the 1953 season.[42] "This winter, I'll do nothing but make sausage," he somewhat jokingly told the press.[43]

While the burgeoning sausage company did take up a good portion of Easter's offseason, he also trained extensively with boxing trainer Freddy Rogers in preparation of the new season. Rogers had been the trainer to heavyweight contender Johnny Risko. Easter beamed about Rogers after their sessions were over. Insisting that his knee did not have to be drained once during his time with Rogers, Easter stated that "I only wish I'd met him a year ago. Things would be different now."[44]

Easter, as he was pictured on his 1953 baseball card from the Bowman Gum Company. The photo was more than likely snapped during his stellar 1952 campaign. (Public Domain)

Easter, in entering the salary negotiations with Greenberg for the 1953 season, was lauded for his 31 home runs on the season.

'Thirty-seven home runs," Easter interjected.

"No, you hit 31 home runs, Luke" Greenberg said.

"You forgot the six I hit in Indianapolis," Easter stated matter-of-factly, widely grinning.[45]

Negotiating for money on his contract was almost like a high-stakes card game for Easter, which he loved. His greatest passion, aside from baseball, was playing cards.

Easter wanted $20,000, which represented a substantial raise of the previous season's rate. Greenberg was initially resistant, but he eventually yielded and gave Easter what he had asked for, admitting "without Luke's fine comeback from Indianapolis last July I don't know where we might have finished," he continued "Mark it down, however, that this is the first time a .263 hitter has worked me for a big raise and it isn't likely to become a habit."[46]

Easter, going toe-to-toe with the shrewd, unflappable Hank Greenberg, had won the staring contest, with Greenberg blinking first.

It was just that kind of year for Luke Easter.

# 11.

## On the Outs

"I got lots of baseball in me yet."

*-Luke Easter, in a conversation with Indians general manager Hank Greenberg before the 1954 season.*

It was a good spring training for Easter in 1953. Short of missing a game for being spiked at first base, he had stayed relatively healthy for the first spring in a couple seasons. He had hit .341 and poled six home runs during exhibition play.[1]

With spring training wrapped up, the Indians made their way back to Cleveland readying themselves for another run at the Bronx Bombers, the New York Yankees, whom the Indians had finished second to in the standings the previous two seasons.

Easter, relaxing at his kitchen table eating his Sunday breakfast, was resting up. Undoubtedly eager to get the season going the following Tuesday against the Chicago White Sox.

Easter peeled the rubber band off the Sunday edition of the *Plain Dealer*. As he unfurled the paper, the headline jumped off the front page, 'THREE BOYS ON BIKES KILLED BY CAR'. Under the headline were pictures of the wreckage of an old Buick, mangled children's bicycles, and three smiling boys, killed in the accident the previous day. Tragic, Easter thought, as he studied the boys' innocent faces. The children were killed by a drunk driver, who would later admit to police he was at the end of a two-day drinking binge. Two were siblings, Fredrick and Peter Allen, ages 12 and 9. The third smiling boy was Daniel A. Jack Jr., nine years old. All three were from Willoughby Township, a Cleveland suburb.

Easter read over the names again and again. His heart sank. He pulled out his billfold and retrieved a simple handwritten letter. It implored him to 'keep your head up through the tough times', signed 'Daniel Jack, Willoughby Township - 8 years old'. Easter stood up, and called for his wife, but he found no words, only tears flowed down the big man's face.[2]

On Tuesday April 14, the Indians opened the season with 6-0 win over the Chicago White Sox, a game where Easter singled twice and drove in the first run of the year. Bob Lemon threw a one-hitter, with his only hit allowed being a first inning Minnie Minoso single.[3] His heart was still heavy for his young fan.

On Wednesday, the Indians had the day off. That morning, Easter climbed into his Buick to pay his respects for his friend Daniel Jack from Willoughby Township. While making the trip to Saint Felicitas Catholic Church in Euclid, Ohio, he had trouble finding the church and got lost in the unfamiliar neighborhood. When he finally found the church, he quietly entered through the backdoor to find that the service had nearly ended.[4]

This was a time when the suburban neighborhood was nearly all-white, making Easter's entrance far from inconspicuous. Identifying Daniel's parents, Easter showed them the note the boy had wrote him ten months earlier. He explained just how much it meant to him when he was struggling with the Indians. "With tears welling in his eyes, the hulking man tried to put into words the devastation he'd felt when he heard the news. He tried to explain how sorry he was for the loss of Daniel, as well as that of the other two boys."[5] The boy's family was eternally grateful for Easter's appearance and kind words during the tragic time.

Four days later, Easter, already hitting .385 with five runs batted in on the young season, was hit on the left foot by White Sox hurler Lou Kretlow on a low fastball. Easter limped all the way to first base and stood for a minute before calling timeout, unable to stand the pain. Easter had broken his foot, and it would be 'at least five or six weeks before (he) could walk again." It was the fourth game of the season.[6] "I went out to check and saw his metatarsal bone was broken," trainer Wally Bock later stated, "He wanted to keep on playing. I can't recall a player with more courage."[7]

Easter had finally realized much of the potential that had been billed to him, but he simply could not outrun his hard luck injuries. After his utterly brilliant 1952 campaign, he lasted exactly four games before suffering another possible long-term injury.

Dejected, manager Al Lopez stated that "Luke had never looked better than he did this spring and he was expecting to have a great season. I only hope he recovers quickly and isn't bothered by the thing all year."[8]

The early reports were that Easter would miss at least two months while recovering and rehabilitating the injury.

After missing 54 games, Easter finally returned to the lineup on June 22. He continued to hit rather effectively, but sported a noticeable limp in his gait and was extremely limited on defense. Through early August, he had only slugged four home runs in 160 plate appearances. The power was nowhere to be found. Through his first three full seasons, Easter averaged a home run every 17 at-bats. Through the first 45 games of the 1953 campaign, his mark stood at one home run every 37.5 at-bats, though he was still hitting at a .287 clip.[9]

The Indians found themselves in familiar territory as well in early August. In second place, looking up at the Yankees. Gayle Talbot of the Associated Press had scathing words for the Cleveland Indians, "Why for instance," he wrote, "Did we persist in believing that the Cleveland Indians had the class and the depth to beat the New York Yankees out of their fifth straight pennant."[10]

He continued in on Easter.

> "In Cleveland's case, why didn't we realize that Luke Easter was too old and too brittle to supply, day in and day out, the kind of power hitting the Indians would need to stick in the race...We realized that the huge first baseman had fudged on his official age and was somewhere around the 37-38 bracket."[11]

Ironically, two days before the words were written, Easter had celebrated his 38th birthday. The day Talbot wrote penned the column, Easter slammed a sixth inning home run off Red Sox hurler Mel Parnell. A week later on August 14, Easter slugged two more home runs in a game with the St. Louis Browns, his sixth and seventh on the season. The shellackings which would prove to be the final clouts on the season for Easter. Hobbled as ever, he would only start nine more games over the final six weeks of the season, appearing in nine others as a pinch hitter.[12]

At season's end, despite having won 92 games, the Indians found themselves in the same spot as seasons past, looking up at the Yankees. The Yankees would win just shy of 100 games, besting the Indians by 8.5 games.[13]

Late in the season, perhaps echoing the sentiments of the entire team, Easter engaged in some banter with legendary Yankee skipper Casey Stengel.

"What are you going to do next year when Mize retires?" Easter shouted at Stengel. Johnny Mize, the famed slugger was 40 years old, and had been with the Yankees since he was 36.

Stengel, not one to back away from a verbal sparring, went with the low-hanging fruit in responding to Easter: age.

"Oh, no," Stengel playfully responded, "We just found out today he's 32 insteadda 40. He'll be around until 1963."[14]

The Indians lost the tilt, 8-5.

Easter would finish with the 1953 campaign with the highest average of his career, .303, though he only started 55 total games (playing in 68). July represented the only month of the season where Easter was able to start double-digit games.[15]

Ironically, it was the same man whom Easter shared a rookie season with that would enjoy the most success of any Indian that year. Al Rosen would have one of the finest seasons by any third baseman in baseball history in 1953. 'Flip' lead the league in runs, home runs, runs batted in, slugging percentage, and total bases. The 29-year old missed winning baseball's Triple Crown by .001

points on his batting average. In a twist of fate, it was former Indian Mickey Vernon who took home the batting title. Rosen would ultimately take home the league's Most Valuable Player honors.[16]

Easter and Rosen, both exceeding rookie limits in 1950, were heading in different directions, career-wise.

One day after the season, Jim Schlemmer of the *Akron Beacon Journal* reported that the Indians were once again shopping Easter's services, even considering putting him on the waiver wire. "Is the Tribe Through with 'Big Luke'?" the headline read.[17]

27-year old Bill Glynn, who played in 147 games (including 135 at first base in Easter's absence) was allegedly a favorite of manager Al Lopez, but he had almost no home run power. Despite the MVP season, Lopez openly contemplated switching Rosen to first base, having publicly bemoaned his defensive abilities at third base. The team had also purchased the rights to 28-year old Rocky Nelson, who had belted 34 home runs and drove in 136 runs in Montreal.[18]

Ultimately, general manager Hank Greenberg would put a pin in a long-term solution for the issue until the start of the 1954 campaign. Luke Easter was nowhere to be found in his long-term plans.

After taking a year off, Easter barnstormed fairly heavily with Jackie Robinson's outfit after the season had ended. Feeling the perilousness of the situation, he clearly wanted to show Greenberg he could still swing the bat. The tour lasted from early-October (after the World Series), through mid-November. Showing a bit of bounce back, Easter hit 20 home runs in 33 exhibition contests.[19]

After the tour had completed, Easter went to Cleveland Municipal Stadium to meet with Greenberg, the entire exchange documented by Harry Jones at the *Plain Dealer*.

"How do you feel Luke? You don't look any different."

"Feel fine. Fact is, I was workin' out this mornin'."

"You worried about next season?" Greenberg asked.

"What I got to be worried 'bout. I'm as happy as a bird singin' up in a tree. No cause to worry at all."

"What tree?" Greenberg asked with a laugh, "There are no birds in my trees. They've all gone...and you'll be gone too."

"I'm not going anywheres," Easter responded with a glare, "I got lots of baseball in me yet."

"You mean because you hit 20 home runs in those exhibition games?" Greenberg asked caustically, "They must have been using golf balls."

After more spirited banter, Greenberg asked the question Easter was expecting.

"So you really think you can play next year, huh? Ever hear of a guy named Rocky Nelson?"

"I heard of him," Luke answered, "I saw him play in a World Series one time. He pinched hit and struck out."

"Now don't go throwing stones at guys who strike out," Greenberg interjected, "You've struck out a few times yourself."

"Oh, I didn't mean it that way," Easter responded, "Fella's a good player from what I hear. He just don't worry me none."

"You know, it's a funny thing. I asked Rocky Nelson if he ever heard of you. He said he did."

Well, if he's heard of ol' Luke I guess I don't worry him none either," Luke replied with a laugh.

"You're all right, Luke," Greenberg finished, "If you could only hit..."[20]

Greenberg really enjoyed Easter, but he was also one of the shrewdest executives in baseball. Perhaps the lunch was a method of letting Easter know his time in Cleveland could be winding down.

In December, Easter opened his second business venture in Cleveland. Easter invited "everybody in town" to the grand opening of 'Luke Easter's Dining Room', in the famed Cleveland Majestic Hotel. Primarily an African American establishment by way of Jim Crow Laws, the Majestic Hotel was the most popular jazz establishment in the city.[21] The restaurant featured fish, pork chops, and steaks with enlarged pictures of Indian players adorning the walls.[22]

The assumption for almost the entirety of the duration the Indians were at their spring training site in Tucson was that Easter would probably at least begin the season in the minor leagues.[23]

"I've been reading in some columns where I'll be a pinch hitter this year," Easter told reporters that spring. "If that's what's best for the club, it'll be okay with me. I figure it will start out that way, but not for long," He confidently finished.[24]

If the reporters were curious if the advent of his new restaurant was going to affect his playing weight, he responded with a pat to his flat stomach, "No fat. Potatoes once a week. Plenty of steak. A piece of pie, just on Sundays."[25]

Mostly due to the spring struggles of Glynn and Nelson, Easter was slated to make the club out of spring training. His case was also bolstered by none other than one of his classic 'Easter Eggs'.

During an April 4 spring training game in Dallas, Texas, Easter slugged a Sal Maglie pitch over the right center field wall for a home run. "The ball left the park at the 373 foot sign but it was then higher than the scoreboard and appeared to be climbing," exclaimed Jim Schlemmer the following day, "Estimates start at 475 feet, with most being over 500."[26]

Despite being hurt for much of spring training, Bill Glynn received the nod to start Opening Day on April 13. Lopez stated the team simply needed "defense and Glynn is a good defensive player," as the rational to start Glynn over Easter.[27] It was the first time since 1950 that Easter would not be the Opening Day first baseman for the Indians.

Easter would receive only six pinch-hitting opportunities, notching one hit on April 15.

On May 12, Easter was released from the Indians active roster and optioned to the Ottawa Athletics of the International League.[28]

The following day, a fan letter was published in the *Akron Beacon Journal*, which only too-aptly described the state:

> Luke Easter
> En Route to Ottawa
>
> Dear Luke:
>
> Fans will always wonder how many pennants the Indians would have won if they hired you and Satchel Paige when you were both in your prime.[29]

On the inside, Easter was sore over the situation. He hadn't felt he was given the chance to prove himself both healthy and productive during the 1954 regular season. Outside, he took it in stride. His wife Vergil, whom he had married a couple years before, says he would tell her 'Babe, I'm not worried. Somebody needs a good hitter," they would then grab a deck a cards, play solitaire and listen for the phone to ring.[30]

In his three most-complete years as an Indian, Easter averaged nearly 30 home runs and 102 runs batted in per season. This included a 'Player of the Year' nod in 1952, while receiving Most Valuable Player consideration in an utterly improbable comeback.

This was, of course, done between the actual age of 33 and 38 for Easter. He was easily among the most productive players of his (actual) age. But, the era would dictate his age for him. Luckily, he was flexible. He signed at a fabled 27, and was cut at perhaps an even more-fabled 32 years of age.

Luke Easter battled a multitude of injuries, beanballs, near-constant booing from the home crowds, racial taunts from opposing teams, a hostile and impatient press corps, and a manager who really never cared for him to thrive as the eleventh player to break the color barrier of Major League Baseball. He generally met his detractors with a calm geniality, while letting his play speak for him.

For a guy who came up 'in the worst of conditions', Easter had performed incredibly.

*Easter, shown here with wife Vergil, packing a suitcase during the early 1950's. (Cleveland Indians team archives)*

# 12.

# What Next?

*"The likable giant was 10 years too late getting into organized baseball, and although the spirit was willing to forget those years, the legs weren't."*[1]

*-1955 Cleveland Indians season preview, predicting Easter's days in organized baseball were finished.*

Though he was originally holding out for an opportunity to return to San Diego and play for the Padres, Easter accepted his assignment with the Ottawa A's of the International League. He arrived on May 18 in the early morning hours with his wife Vergil his two-month old son Gerald in-tow.[2]

Edward MacCabe, A's beat writer was there to greet him when he arrived in town at 2:00am. The writer asked Easter a bevy of questions, and also shared a quote that Casey Stengel had said about Easter the week before, "They won't win without him. He's more dangerous on one leg than most guys with two."

Easter responded, "Case is a great old fellow."[3]

Also being one for a good story, Easter shared how he got his start in baseball with MacCabe, while also promulgating the myth he didn't play baseball until 1945.

"I was in Chicago then, and there was this sandlot team. I asked the manager if I could play. He asked where I played and I said anywhere, and he said anybody who plays anywhere can't play baseball."

Easter continued, "So I told him I could do better than most of the fellows out there but he says no. Well, I begged and begged and finally he let me play, and in the first game I hit two homers."[4]

Luke Easter, always good for spinning a yarn at two o'clock in the morning after an eight-hour drive.

Easter made his debut as a member of the Ottawa A's that evening on May 18, walking twice, grounding out, and being hit by a pitch.[5]

By the start of June, Easter's average had swelled to well over .300. He slugged a home run during a June 3 contest against the Havana Sugar Kings that completely left the stadium, bouncing on an adjoining street.[6]

A June 25 dugout altercation between Easter and Athletics manager Les Bell netted the first baseman a suspension and a $100 fine. Bell had accused Easter of not hustling defensively, to which Easter took exception.[7]

It was no secret Easter wasn't thrilled to be in Ottawa, where the average temperature is much colder than in Cleveland, which made his knees ache. On July 14, the Indians optioned him over to the San Diego Padres, his original preference.[8] He was slated to return to the place he had spent nearly the entire 1949 campaign at.

His tenuous tenure in Ottawa was complete. Between mid-May and June, Easter appeared in 66 games for the Athletics. He hit well, .348, slugging 15 home runs and driving in 48 runs. He also took 42 walks as opposed to striking out only 38 times.[9]

Easter celebrated his July 18 return to San Diego by hitting a 490-foot blast on his first day back in a Padres uniform.[10]

He hit four more in day-night doubleheader that got successively longer with each blast, according to *The San Bernadino County Sun* on August 8.[11]

Altogether, between Ottawa and San Diego, Easter would play in 122 games, hitting .315 (collecting 135 total hits), including 28 home runs and 90 runs batted in. If it were anything like previous seasons, the struggling second-place Indians, desperate for a late offensive surge to overtake the New York Yankees, would come calling.

However, 1954 was not anything like past seasons. The Indians, without Easter in the lineup, would go on to win a Major League Baseball record 111 games that year, an astounding 68 games over .500. Despite the Yankees winning 97 games also, they found themselves trailing the Indians by an insurmountable 14 games. It was the absolute best team the Indians had ever fielded, and they utterly ran away with the pennant that season.

Glynn had started the year at first base, then Rosen came over, then back to Glynn, and then Rosen once more. On June 1, the team acquired right fielder Vic Wertz from the St. Louis Browns, and quickly converted him to a first baseman. In 94 games with the Indians, the 29-year old Wertz hit .275 with 14 home runs and 48 runs batted in, all while playing solid enough first base. Bobby Avila would go on to win the American League batting championship with a .341 average.[12]

The Indians would be swept in the 1954 World Series by the New York Giants, led by former Negro Leaguer Willie Mays. It was during the 1954 version of the Fall Classic where Mays made perhaps one of the best, and famous, plays of baseball history. After a long fly was hit to dead center field, coincidentally off the bat of Wertz, Mays raced back to the wall in a full sprint, outstretching his glove to corral the baseball. Mays quickly spun and threw the ball back to the infield to hold the runners on-base. Despite the tremendous regular season, the Indians were swept by the Giants 4-0.

For his part, albeit a small one, Easter received a $1,000 share of the World Series bonus from the Indians.[13]

On October 14, the Indians sold their rights to Easter to the Indianapolis Indians, essentially severing any and all ties between the player and his former club as far as a comeback to the big league club. Among the players whose contracts was purchased to take Easter's place? 21-year old Bronx native Rocco 'Rocky' Colavito, who would become one of the most beloved players in team history through the rest of the decade and into the 1960's.[14]

When the annual minor league draft occurred on November 22, 3,640 minor leaguers hoped their names would be called by a big league club, including Easter. In an era with no amateur draft, the rights to minor league players could be bought and negotiated by their parent clubs. Easter's name, however, was not called in the proceedings.[15] Easter proceeded to play ball in the Mexican Winter League.[16] He led the league in home runs with 20.[17]

In January of 1955, the double-A Charleston Senators, of Charleston, West Virginia, acquired Easter from the Indianapolis Indians. The Senators front office announced that Easter's signing "coupled with Clyde Vollmer, the Senators now offer for the first time as fine a one-two home run punch as exists in the minors today." Vollmer was a 10-year veteran with 69 big league home runs under his belt.[18]

The Senators' spring training site was in Fort Pierce, Florida. For the first time that had at least been recorded in the previous several seasons, Easter would not be wearing his customary number nine jersey, instead opting for number 28.[19]

Once the regular season opened, Easter immediately began to power the Senators. On the team's April 19 contest, Easter hit a grand slam en route to driving in a whopping eight runs in a 17-7 Senators victory.[20]

Two days later, Easter was a single short of a cycle as he doubled, tripled, and stroked a 450-foot home run in a Senators defeat.[21] Another home run followed a few days later.[22]

Just as they had in the past, Easter's new teammates loved him. The community of Charleston was embracing the big first baseman as well. After a Charleston Kiwanis Club 'baseball day' luncheon, Easter put on a hitting display for the locals, hitting no less than a dozen home runs in a few minute span. He'd also throw parties for his Senator teammates. He'd drive his Cadillac over to Cleveland on off-days, and return with a trunk-full of his best poultry his sausage company, packed in dry ice.[23]

Through 14 games with the Senators, Easter had already drove in 21 runs. There was even talk of him approaching the 20-year league record of 154 by season's end.[24]

Easter was not able to keep up his torrid pace, but that didn't mean the season wasn't proving interesting. The Senators who would prove lowly despite Easter's hitting, were playing the St. Paul Saints on June 25. Walt Moryn, Saints right fielder, roped a fly ball down the line, called a foul ball by umpire John Mullen. Saints manager Max Macon immediately came out to argue the validity of Mullen's call.

Among Macon's yelling, Easter called out, "Let the umpire call it." The already-perturbed Macon made a beeline for the big first baseman, landing a soft blow to the left side of his head. Fisticuffs ensued. Both men were ejected and escorted to their respective clubhouses by St. Paul policemen. There was no word on how many blows Easter landed.[25] Sadly, only 1,036 fans were present to witness the spectacle.[26]

Three days after Easter's 40th birthday, he slugged his 26th home run on the season.[27]

On August 18th, it was announced that the slugger had been suspended indefinitely by the team. His crimes? Throwing baseballs to kids in the stands, and opening the gate to the field and letting kids in the playing area after a game had concluded. An additional problem arose when general manager Danny Menendez couldn't locate Easter to serve him his suspension.[28]

The eventful season finally wound down. Easter finished hitting .283 belting 30 home runs and driving in 102 runs on the season for the 50-104 Senators.[29] His 30 round trippers tied him third on the circuit with the upstart Rocky Colavito. Easter, despite some drama, proved to be one of the few bright spots for a team that had finished 42 games back from first place.

On October 19, it was announced that Easter had been sold to the Buffalo Bisons of the International League.[30]

Provided the 40-year old would make the team the following season, he would be the black player to suit up for the Bisons in 67 years.

## 13.

## International League Royalty

*"I just hit 'em and forget 'em"*

*-Luke Easter, when talking about his monstrous home runs as a member of the Buffalo Bisons*

Frank Grant was the last black ballplayer to play for the Buffalo Bisons, which he did from 1886 through 1888.[1] After Easter was passed for the second consecutive year on the minor league draft, it was all but ensured he would break the nearly seven decade-long drought, as he was added to the Bisons active roster.[2]

The Bisons had been affiliated with the Detroit Tigers for most of the previous 15 years. After the 1955 season, the Tigers ended their partnership with the Bisons after consecutive sixth-place seasons in 1954 and 1955 and some the worst attendance figures in the league (about 120,000 per year). The Tigers actually tried to sell the team after the season to another Major League Baseball club, but to no avail. On the surface, it appeared as though baseball in Buffalo, New York was on the verge of extinction.[3]

With the organization in dire straits, longtime team executive John C. Stiglmeier enlisted the aid of a local businessman Harry Bisgeier to help the save the nearly 70-year old franchise. They concocted the idea of the Bisons being community-owned, financed by offering stock to the fans at one dollar per share. Of the 250,000 shares they offered, 182,000 were sold; more than enough to at least cover the $75,000 asking price to buy the team outright from the Tigers.[4]

The purchase of the team was successful, but a new problem arose. For the $75,000 tendered, Stiglmeier and Bisgeier only received the team and the nine players most considered expendable by the Tigers. The Bisons did not have a working relationship with a parent club, so players of substance were certainly going to be hard to come by. Being cash-strapped, the new owners were going to have to be a bit creative in filling their roster. They decided to take a gamble on the wobbly knees of Luke Easter.[5]

Easter had spent the previous months (once again) terrorizing the pitching of the Puerto Rican Winter League, hitting .356 and leading the league (once again) in home runs with 17.[6] He could be the perfect gate attraction, Stiglmeier reasoned, a player who's reputation as a long ball hitter would proceed him, while also becoming the team's first black ball player in the 20th century. He helped break the barrier in the Pacific Coast League and Major League Baseball. Buffalo should be a piece of cake, Stiglmeier reasoned. In an effort to 'build a team to fit Offermann Stadium," Stiglmeier was also thinking of the right field home run porch, which sat a mere 297 feet down the line.[7]

The Bisons scored when they were ultimately able to get the 40-year old Easter to sign a $7,500 pact to play the 1956 season on February 27.[8][9]

The Bisons played their home games at Offermann Stadium. The stadium, originally built in 1924, was originally named 'Bison Stadium' until 1935, when the field was renamed for recently deceased team president, Frank Offermann. The stadium was built to accommodate 13,000 spectators.[10]

Easter appears to have arrived in Buffalo in late March, early April. In one of his first workouts with the club, his teammates marveled as Easter planted seven pitches over the wall during batting practice.[11]

The 1956 version of the Bisons offense would feature six former Major Leaguers in their starting lineup, including Easter, Clyde Vollmer (who played with Easter in Charleston the season before), Billy Mars, Bill Serena, Johnny Blatnik, and Lou Ortiz.[12] The season opener was against the Miami Marlins on April 18.[13]

Luke started the season slow, hitting only .195 through the first 14 games. Easter attributed the struggles to not swinging his traditional 38 ounce bats, which would have easily been among the heaviest in baseball at the time. Easter made a trip to Cleveland himself to pick-up his personal bats. Bisons manager Phil Cavraretta explained that Easter, using too light a bat, was swinging out too far in front of the ball. In his first game with his own bats, Easter hit a home run and two singles.[14] Four days later, two more followed in a game against the Cuban Sugar Kings.[15]

Another culprit to the slower start was Easter's vision. He had been suffering from headaches and blurred vision for years. He was finally fitted for glasses, and he also attributed his new spectacles for his rediscovered success at the plate.[16]

A month into the season, even after the slow start, Easter had belted five home runs for the Bisons.[17] By the end of May, he was tied in the International League lead with nine.[18]

By mid-June, Easter was a full-fledged terror on International League pitching. He had taken the league lead in home runs with 12,[19] and opposing managers where letting him know they weren't too pleased. While waiting outside the batter's box during a June game Easter was taking practice cuts while Rochester Red Wings pitcher Ed Mayer finished his warm-up tosses. The final pitch plunked Easter square in the shoulder. Easter angrily grabbed his bat and started towards Dixie Walker, the Red Wings manager. Though the two were separated, Easter waited for Walker after the game between the clubhouses. Walker snuck away undetected.[20] Easter said he later heard Walker yell out to Mayer to "knock that big so-and-so down."[21]

In mid-July, Easter was selected to the International League All-Star game (they would play the Milwaukee Braves). Easter, hitting .296, had belted 19 home runs and driven in 56 runs.[22]

In Buffalo, the crowds were starting to love their new first baseman. Among the adoring fans in the crowd was young Tim Russert, who would later become a prolific television journalist. "Most International League players were hoping to make it to the major leagues, but a few including...Luke Easter had already been there," he continued "When he came to Buffalo in 1956, his power hitting, and his outgoing personality helped save the franchise."[23]

When Easter would come up to the plate, the crowd would yell "Luuuuuuuuuke", not to be confused with the 'boos' he had often received in Cleveland. Bisons radio announcer Bill Mazer would in fact remind the listening audience that Easter was not the recipient of boos, "Folks, they're not booing," he would say, "They *love* Luke Easter!"[24]

On August 5, Easter celebrated his 41st birthday, as well as hitting his 25th home run on the season in 3-2 win over the Cubans.[25]

He hit another home run the following day, again against the Cubans, which was talked about for years by Buffalo fans. "The blow cleared the right-field light tower, crossed Woodlawn Avenue, soared 30 feet over a two-story dwelling, struck the roof of a house on Emerson Place, the next street over, and finally came to rest in the street. Counting the roll," Bisons historian Joe Overfield said, "It had traveled 550 feet."[26]

Easter would finish out the 1956 season with a .306 batting average. He would lead the entire league in home runs (35), runs batted in (106) and total bases (279).[27] Though the Bisons finished in last place, and over 20 games behind the first place Toronto Maple Leafs, Easter "helped capture the city's interest for the game with countless public appearances, a crucial task for a community-owned team."[28] Attendance also rose nearly 36% over the previous season.[29]

After one year of independence, the community-owned Bisons would ink a partnership with the Kansas City Athletics for the 1957 season.

Heading into the 1957 season, the long balls kept coming in bunches for the big first baseman. A mere month into the campaign, Easter had already socked nine out of the park. The Bisons found themselves in recently-uncharted ground towards the end of May, in first place.[30]

Wholly unexpectedly, the traditional cellar-dwelling Bisons continued to stick near the top of the standings through mid-June. Easter hit his league-leading 18th circuit clout on the 12th.[31]

A couple days later, Easter flat-out rocked the home crowd at Offermann Stadium, giving the good folks of Buffalo something they had never seen before.

In the mid-1950's, the centerfield wall at Offermann was exactly 420 feet from home plate. Towering over the centerfield wall was a 40-foot scoreboard, among the largest in the minor leagues. In nearly four decades, and thousands of contests at all levels, no hitter had ever cleared the scoreboard with a batted ball. Bob Thurman (a former teammate of Easter from the Homestead Grays) had come the closest while playing for the Newark Bears in 1949, but his ball had hit the advertisement at the very top of the board.[32]

On June 14, Easter ambled up to bat during the fourth inning of the second game of a double-header against the Columbus Jets. Bob Kuzava, formerly of the Yankees. Easter had faced him 11 times as a member of the Indians. The most success he had drawn from Kuzava was an RBI walk back in Easter's banner 1952 campaign.

Overfield, who was present for the game, described the scene:

> "The explosion occurred on the evening of June 14, 1957. It was mild and windless, and there was a trace of haze in the air. In the fourth inning of the second game of the evening's double-header, Columbus pitcher Bob Kuzava delivered what he later called 'a perfect pitch' – a knee-high fastball on the outside of the plate. Easter swung, timed the pitch perfectly and sent it soaring high and deep to centerfield. As the ball disappeared into the haze, there was a mighty roar from the crowd as many fans realized what had happened: Luke Easter had just become the first batter ever to hit a ball over the centerfield scoreboard. As Easter completed his home run trot, dead-pan all the

way, the cheering and applause reached decibel levels never previously attained in the old park."[33]

It was concluded that the ball had traveled 550 feet. Unlike his previous shot of the same distance, this one did not include a bounce. After the game was over, Easter boldly predicted "If my legs hold out, I'll do it again." Wouldn't you know it, the very next month he walloped another one over the scoreboard.[34]

Russert, who had witnessed one of the incredible blasts, described the scene through the lens of a young boy, enthralled with the amazing feats of Easter, and where his long balls eventually landed:

> "I used to wonder: What happened? Did it shatter a windshield? Hit somebody's roof? The next morning, I couldn't wait to check the sports pages and read how far the ball had traveled. When the game was over and the crowd filed out of the park, people were still buzzing about Luke's home run. 'Did you *see* that ball?' Fans were smiling from ear to ear."[35]

By the end of July, Easter had smashed 30 home runs and had paced the underdog Bisons to near the top of the standings.[36] The Bisons, the annual cellar dwellers were gearing up for an improbable run.

When the final bell rang on the season, Easter had once again led the league in home runs with 40, and runs batted in with 127. At age 42, Easter had set career highs in both. Also for the first time in his career, Easter had played in every contest, appearing in all 154 games.[37] The Bisons, only a half-game behind the Toronto Maple Leafs in the standings, had largely defied odds to qualify for the International League playoffs.[38]

In the semifinal round, the Bisons eliminated the Richmond Virginians four games to two. Easter hit three home runs in the playoff series.[39,40]

The Bisons had made it to the International League Championship. Awaiting them was none other than the Miami

Marlins, who had clipped the Maple Leafs in their semifinal round. On the Marlins roster was Easter's old teammate and associate Satchel Paige.

After a Bisons 2-0 victory in game one, game two of the series was highlighted by a verbal sparring contest between the old friends. Easter, who was a bit hobbled and had been nursing a bum ankle called out to Paige, who was on the mound, "Satch, I came off the hospital bed when I heard you was goin' to pitch. I was anxious to get a shot at a sure thing even on one leg." Satchel sourly replied, "I wouldn't be pitchin' today, man, if it wasn't for you. As long as I hear you're in baseball I'll keep pickin' up that pitcher's mitt and getting you out. I know a sure thing too."[41]

The Paige-Easter 'feud' was nothing new to the International League. The two had been at it for years; former Marlin Bob Bowman recalled a time when Easter hit a long home run off Paige and "Satch followed him around the bases, yelling at him all around the bases, but good-naturedly." Another former Marlin Ray Semproch recalled, "I'll tell you one thing, he (Paige) and Easter used to go at it. I'll tell you, that was funny. The people used to love it because he would holler at Luke, 'Here comes a curveball. Hit it Luke.' We had a lot of fun. Oh yeah, those two, I'll tell you, it was like Laurel and Hardy."[42]

The Bisons delivered the knockout blow to the Marlins in game five, a 7-1 victory. Luke Easter and the Bisons were the almost implausible International League Champions.[43]

Baseball had been successfully revived in Buffalo, New York. The newly-crowned champions were not only victorious on the diamond, but also at the turnstiles. Attendance skyrocketed to a whopping 386,071. This was not only the best mark in all minor league baseball, it also represented an over 300% increase from the annual gate number before Easter arrived in Buffalo.[44]

Easter would hit another 38 home runs and drive in another 109 runs the following season in 1958. Ironically, he finished second in both categories to Rocky Nelson, the first baseman whose career never quite panned out after he was allegedly taking Easter's spot as the Indians' first sacker.

Before the 1959 season, the Bisons inked a deal with the Philadelphia Phillies to be their new parent club. With the change, came a youth movement for the Bisons. Frank Herrera was the heir apparent first baseman for the Phillies. With respect to Easter, the team tried Herrera at third and second before finally placing him permanently at first base. On May 14, Easter was given his formal release from the Bisons. In his three seasons in Buffalo, Easter hit 113 home runs and drove in 343 runs with a .297 average. More importantly, he had undoubtedly helped save baseball in the city.[45]

The *Buffalo Courier-Express* relayed the headline "THERE IS NO JOY, LUKE IS RELEASED" on the fateful day, undoubtedly mirroring fan sentiment.[46]

Seizing the opportunity, Easter was quickly signed by another International League franchise, the Rochester Red Wings, mere days later.

For the rest of the 1959 season, Easter would club 22 more improbable home runs and drive in 76 runs for the Red Wings as a 44-year old.[47]

His reputation certainly proceeded him. Every time Easter came up to bat, the traditional 'Luuuuuuke', 'Luuuuuuke' chant served as a precursor. Though much of his home run-hitting power was gone after the 1959 campaign, the fans, particularly the children, still adored him.[48]

Once, a young fan nervously approached Easter to ask for an autograph. Never one to turn down a child, Easter scribbled his name on the child's piece of paper, smiling down at him as he returned it to him. The child looked at his hero, awestruck.

"Mr. Easter," the boy said nervously. "I saw your longest home run"

Easter looked down at the boy, facetiously responding: "Did you see it land?"

"Yes sir. I saw it land way over the fence and..."

With a wide grin on his face, he softly interjected, "Bub, if you saw it land, you didn't see my longest home run."[49]

Towards the end of the 1960 season, Easter's first full season as a Red Wing, the team threw 'Luke Easter Night' at the ballpark to commemorate the 45-year old legend. More than eight thousand fans attended. Easter was showered with gifts such as a "color television set, fishing equipment, a $300 dollar wrist watch with diamond numerals, a movie camera, luggage, and even a frozen turkey and five pounds of sausage."[50] Easter loved the validation he received from fans. He graciously accepted the gifts from the fans and organization. As he did so, tears were streaming down his cheeks.[51]

Between 1960 and 1963, Easter would only play in 367 games (or roughly 92 games per year). Though he would only hit 45 home runs over that span, Red Wings fans would often sit and wait through lopsided victories or defeats in hopes that Easter would enter the game for a pinch-hitting appearance. "Easter was possibly the most beloved Red Wing of all time, a gentle giant of a man who was entertaining to watch even when he was striking out, which he did often," a Red Wings team history reported.[52] Even in his mid-forties, and nowhere near the peak of his game, he was still the most popular player in the entire circuit.[53]

Easter's kindness was always on display. Rochester writer George Beahon wrote, "Foul weather or fair, he never denied an autograph. During those years, after I filed stories from the press box to the morning paper, I would see Luke still around the clubhouse or the parking lot, signing his name and making friends for the franchise."[54]

Bob Matthews, a longtime columnist and radio personality for Rochester-area sports, once said, "In the early-1960's, I was convinced Luke Easter was the greatest man alive."[55]

For his years in Rochester, Easter was named to their inaugural team Hall of Fame class of 1989.

In 1964, just before his 49th birthday, Luke Easter decided to hang up his cleats for good. Interestingly enough, when asked about his age, Easter claimed to be 53 that season, four years older than he actually was. After nearly three decades in baseball, consistently dodgy with his actual age during most of those, Easter insisted he was actually *older* than he was. "Aw, that 1921 is just my playing birthday. I started playing with the St. Louis Giants in 1933-and I don't think I made it that high when I was only 12. I guess I was born about 1911."[56] Well, Easter was nothing if not flexible with these types of matters.

Easter would stick around Rochester through the 1965 season. He would help coach the Red Wings that season and make several publicity appearances for the team as well. He even ran for political office in Rochester's third ward, but was defeated by nearly a two-to-one margin.[57]

Easter would finally move back to the place he most considered home throughout his baseball life, Cleveland, Ohio, with his wife Vergil.[58]

After a few years away from baseball, Easter received a phone call from Gabe Paul, general manager of the Indians. He wanted Easter to join the team for two weeks during spring training as a member of the coaching staff, with plans to be on the bench during the regular season as well. The plan was for Easter to serve the team during the regular season for home games only, that way he could keep his position at the local Thompson Ramo Woolridge (TRW) plant.[59] He had actually begun on the nightshift, polishing airplane parts, but he had gained the trust and confidence of his co-workers to the extent that he was soon named chief steward of the Aircraft Worker's Alliance.

In agreeing to help the Indians, Easter became the first black coach in Cleveland Indians history (Frank Robinson would eventually become the first black manager in baseball when becoming the skipper for the Tribe in 1975), and only the fourth black coach overall, following Jim Gillam, Gene Baker, and Buck O'Neil.[60] Upon hearing the news that he was being hired as coach, Easter gathered his family around (with the exception of son Terry, who was a Division II basketball player for Saint Martin's University in Washington), telling them "Such a thrill you hardly ever get in life. It'll be just like putting on a big league suit for the first time." Suffice to say, Easter was thrilled to be back in baseball.[6162]

*Easter suited as the first black coach in Cleveland Indians history, 1969. (Cleveland Indians team archives)*

Easter's old teammate Al 'Flip' Rosen was also thrilled to have Easter back in the baseball fold, "Luke is a really magnificent, warm, wonderful human being. Just a fine man. He never asked for a thing in his life. He didn't ask for this. It was marvelous of Gabe Paul to give Luke a break." As it turned out, Easter was only 109 days from earning his five-year Major League Baseball pension.[63]

Easter always loved Rosen; in the same article about Easter landing the coaching position, Rosen retold the story when Luke was cheering so intensely after a walk-off home run from Rosen, that he jumped a bit too high in the dugout, knocking himself out temporarily on the concrete ceiling. When the rest of the team returned to the dugout, they found the giant Easter laying on the floor.

After the 1969 season, Easter would never work in baseball again. He would make many public appearances over the years, always for a just social cause; he spoke to Rotary Clubs, adult education centers, to convicts in prison, all while stressing it was never too late to start a new life for yourself or make a difference in others.[64]

Easter often found himself participating in old-timers games with former Bob Feller, and others such as Warren Spahn, Pee Wee Reese, Stan Musial, Mickey Mantle, among many others.[65]

But mostly, Easter just lived a normal life. He had experienced so much time in the limelight, a peaceful existence just seemed to suit him a bit better. He settled back into his position at TRW, where he was intent on eventually retiring.

# Conclusion
## March 29, 1979

It was not unlike any other payday. The 63-year old Luke Easter, dutifully serving in his role as the union steward, was carrying a bag full of checks to cash for his co-workers; a role which he routinely filled for less-tenured employees who may not have had the flexibility during the work day to get their paychecks cashed. True, selfless, Luke Easter form.

Easter had worked for TRW for almost 15 years. He had served as the union steward for the previous nine. What began as a fairly innocuous task, cashing a paycheck for a co-worker, had grown into quite the endeavor; dozens of employees at the plant trusted Easter with their hard-earned livelihood, and he was happy to return their trust with a timely delivery of their paychecks.

On March 29, 1979, Easter was entrusted with nearly $40,000 of his co-workers paychecks.[1]

Sometimes he would get suspicious that he was being followed on his way to or from the bank with the checks or cash. He would often call the police and be granted an escort, a task the local law enforcement was often more than happy to oblige, given his regional celebrity. Whether he had an escort or not, he always kept a small revolver in a pocket inside his jacket, just in case.

When Easter disappeared into the Cleveland Bank and Trust on Euclid Avenue that morning, he certainly would not have known he was being watched. The two strangers in a car across the street were subtle enough that the old ballplayer would not have suspected a thing. One of the men was a former, disgruntled employee of TRW and was already aware of Easter's arrangement with his co-worker's checks.[2]

A few minutes later Easter emerged from the bank with a canvas sack, ostensibly filled with cash, the men reasoned. As Easter walked to his car, the strangers threw their own car in drive, cutting off Easter before he could reach his vehicle. The two men emerged from their vehicle and accosted Easter, pointing a sawed-off shotgun and a revolver at him, demanding he turn over the money. Easter would have undoubtedly recognized one of the men as a former TRW employee.[3]

Inside the bank, a loan officer who was watching the events unfold, picked up a phone to call the police.[4]

Easter, may have been caught off-guard, but was not probably surprised by the turn of events. He refused to turn over the money and quickly made a move for his own hidden revolver. However, before he could draw the weapon, a loud blast rang out. The strangers quickly gathered as much cash as they could and took off in their getaway car. Easter, struck in the chest at point-blank range by the shotgun, fell to the ground.

An ambulance was called, and soon arrived, but it was too late. Luke Easter, the man who never met a stranger, who would have obliged his assailants had they asked for the clothes off his very back, was dead.

Easter's assailants were quickly apprehended by the police, their pockets stuffed full of stolen cash. Surrounding Easter's body was nearly $30,000 of his co-worker's money and his old revolver.[5]

The city mourned the sudden and tragic loss of their hero. More than 1,000 people packed Mt. Sinai Baptist Church to pay their last respects to their fallen hero. During the calling at the funeral home, nearly 4,000 people turned out.[6]

"You have come to pay homage to a man who will never die," Reverend Luther Hill told the funeral assembly, "Easter was a living example of the power of love. A man who couldn't say 'no' to pleas for help, who wouldn't turn down a needy person."[7]

Former teammates Bob Cain, Mike Garcia, Al Rosen, and Bob Lemon served as pallbearers at the funeral. At the time of his death, he was survived by his wife Vergil, six children and three grandchildren.[8]

Tributes poured in. Bill Veeck, the Indians owner who originally signed Easter said "Two creeps with guns. They were the only two people alive who didn't love Luke Easter."[9]

His co-workers at TRW beamed about his ability to make everyone in the organization feel special, each in their own individual way, and that he was constantly smiling."[10]

*Plain Dealer* sports editor Hal Lebovitz wrote that, "I loved him - like a brother. Anyone who knew him did. Cleveland lost a civic asset." Lebovitz continued on the unfortunate timing of Easter's baseball brilliance, "One wonders what Luke's major league record would have been had there been no racial barrier in the majors and he had been able to start at a young age. With his power, no telling how many records he would have broken. He had more power than anyone I ever saw."[11]

Another tribute that came in was from Ken MacKenzie of Muncie, Indiana. He wanted Easter's family to know how much it meant to him and his own family when Easter appeared at his cousin Daniel Jack's funeral all those years ago, to show his sympathy and express his gratitude to the young boy he had never met, but had wrote him a heartfelt, uplifting fan letter. MacKenzie wanted to relay how much that helped the family gain closure during the tragic affair, during which Daniel and his two friends were killed by a drunk driver while riding their bicycles. "Luke Easter, I learned later, was idolized by Danny Jack. Luke had his best year in 1952, but was in a slump in 1953 and many fans were down on him. Not Danny Jack. He wrote letters to his idol asking him to hang in there; slump or no slump, he was behind him all the way."[12]

The letter finished, "I suspect that many, as I, shall never forget Luke..."[13]

A tribute from an older Rochester Red Wings fan also arrived. In a simple letter to the editor of the *Democrat and Chronicle*, it stated:

"Perhaps it was his size. Perhaps it was his gentleness and good humor that offset and, at the same time, complemented his power.

More than anything, it was his age. Here was a man who somehow succeeded in doing what our parents warned us could never be done – he had played a child's game all his life and played each game with the joy that accompanies our first schoolyard game after a long winter.

We admired him especially for his diminishing skills; with every at-bat, the odds against his success grew. Yet the possibility of success made the anticipation, and its fulfillment, all the more rewarding.

When we read that Luke Easter died, our childhood dreams also seemed to die – for all of us who hoped to remain children a little longer."[14]

The title of the poignant prose? "Folk Hero Forever".

A year after Easter's death, the former Woodland Hills Park on Cleveland's east side was renamed Luke Easter Park in his honor. Shortly after, a bust of Easter was unveiled, with the words "Strong, Courageous and Beloved as a Baseball Player and as a Man" were inscribed on the memorial.

Though Easter's life was tragically ended less than 15 miles away from the park, it's only fitting that Easter's bust, situated in the city he loved most, still smiles from ear to ear.

## Appendix A

## "A Yearly Log of 'Easter Eggs'"

By the time Easter actually retired, he could be credited with at least 650 professional home runs. Every long ball in the count was recorded during and after the season which Easter turned 31 years old. This would not count any of his home runs on barnstorming tours, or any hit before joining the Cincinnati Crescents in 1946. The numbers are strictly those in 'league' play (exhibition played within the timeframe of the regular season, or in a competitive foreign offseason league). All statistics accessed from BaseballReference.com unless stated otherwise:

| Year(s) | Team | League | # of HRs |
| --- | --- | --- | --- |
| 1946 | Cincinnati Crescents | Independent Negro | 74[1] |
| 1946 | Cincinnati Crescents | Hawaiian Fall League | 12[2] |
| 1947 | Homestead Grays | Negro National League | 43[3] |
| 1947-48 | Patriotas de Venezuela | Venezuelan Winter League | 8[4] |
| 1948 | Homestead Grays | Negro National League | 56[5] |
| 1949 | San Diego Padres | Pacific Coast League | 25 |
| 1948-50 | Indios de Mayaguez | Puerto Rican Winter League | 48[6] |
| 1950 | Cleveland Indians | Major League Baseball | 28 |
| 1951 | Cleveland Indians | Major League Baseball | 37 |
| 1952 | Cleveland Indians | Major League Baseball | 31 |
| 1952 | Indianapolis Indians | International League | 6 |
| 1953 | Cleveland Indians | Major League Baseball | 7 |
| 1954 | Ottawa Senators | International League | 15 |
| 1954 | San Diego Padres | Pacific Coast League | 13 |
| 1954-55 | Queliteros de Hermosillo | Mexican Winter League | 20[7] |
| 1955 | Charleston Senators | American Association | 30 |
| 1955-56 | Leones de Ponce | Puerto Rican Winter League | 17[8] |
| 1956 | Buffalo Bisons | International League | 35 |
| 1957 | Buffalo Bisons | International League | 40 |
| 1958 | Buffalo Bisons | International League | 38 |
| 1959 | Rochester Red Wings | International League | 22 |
| 1960 | Rochester Red Wings | International League | 14 |
| 1961 | Rochester Red Wings | International League | 10 |
| 1962 | Rochester Red Wings | International League | 15 |
| 1963 | Rochester Red Wings | International League | 6 |
| 1964 | Rochester Red Wings | International League | 0 |

# Appendix B

## "That Famous Card Shark Story"

Luke Easter loved to play cards. There has been a story that has been told in a truncated fashion regarding Easter winning back his teammates money from a crooked gambler while a member of the Indians. The story was originally told by Hal Lebovitz of the *Cleveland Plain Dealer*, and is worth repeating, for it tells a lot about the character of Easter. The anecdote, in its entirety, was printed in Lebovitz's book *The Best of Hal Lebovitz: Great Sportswriting from Six Decades in Cleveland,* originally published in 2004:

"The Indians had finished a series in Boston and took the night train to Detroit. Attached to the regular train were several cars transporting soldiers to their base.

The soldiers went into the club car where several Indians were sitting around having a few beers and playing cards. Soon, the conductor chased them out, saying they didn't have club car privileges. Two strangers remained. Apparently, they boarded the train for the sole purpose of fleecing the soldiers. They became friendly with Early Wynn.

Soon, Wynn excused himself to get into the poker game with teammate Bob Lemon, Harry Simpson, Easter, and a few others. Minutes later, the strangers asked if they could join. The players thought they were friends of Wynn and said okay.

Wynn lost a bundle quickly and became a spectator. He noticed the strangers were seated so they had the players trapped between raises. The strangers did most of the winning and Wynn suddenly was certain he saw one dealing from the bottom of the deck.

He screamed and grabbed the man. As soon as he did, the other stranger ran out of the club car. Wynn held his victim and appeared about to throttle him when big Luke stepped in.

'Hold it, Early,' he said. 'If you hurt this guy, you could get in trouble. Man, sit down. You and I are going to play gin."

The stranger had no choice. Luke sat opposite him while the others watched. In short order, Luke had won back all the money – and more.

'Get out of here,' he told the stranger. 'Don't ever let us see you again.' The man left – fast.

Luke asked Lemon, Wynn and the others how much they had lost and gave them back the precise amount.

Later, I asked him, 'Luke, how could you play against a man who deals from the bottom of the deck and still be so sure you're going to win?'

He laughed. 'I can deal from the middle of the deck,' he said.

I wanted to write this priceless anecdote, but Luke asked me to hold off. 'Al Lopez (the manager) won't let us play for more than a 25-cent limit,' he said. 'If you run it, he'll fine all of us. You can print it after I'm no longer with the team.'

He finally gave me permission a year later."

## Appendix C

## "The First Dozen: A Timeline of Baseball Integration"

### *1947*

April 15 – Jackie Robinson debuts for the Brooklyn Dodgers

July 5 – Larry Doby debuts for the Cleveland Indians

July 17 – Hank Thompson debuts for the St. Louis Browns

July 19 – Willard Brown debuts for the St. Louis Browns

August 26 – Dan Bankhead debuts for the Brooklyn Dodgers

### *1948*

April 20 – Roy Campanella debuts for the Brooklyn Dodgers

July 8 – Satchel Paige debuts for the Cleveland Indians

### *1949*

April 19 – Minnie Minoso debuts for the Cleveland Indians

May 20 – Don Newcombe debuts for the Brooklyn Dodgers

July 8 – Monte Irvin debuts for the New York Giants

August 11 – Luke Easter debuts for the Cleveland Indians

### *1950*

April 18 – Sam Jethroe debuts for the Boston Braves

Among the first 12 black baseball players, six (Robinson, Doby, Brown, Campanella, Paige, and Irvin) have been elected to the Baseball Hall of Fame.

Three (Robinson, Newcombe, and Jethroe) were named Major League Baseball's 'Rookie of the Year'.

Two (Easter and Campanella) were named the *Sporting News* Player of the Year Award.

Altogether, they were named to a total of 37 All-Star games, with Minoso (9 selections), Campanella (8), and Doby (7) leading the way.

## Bibliography

### Books/Scholarly Articles

Beck, Peggy. *Working in the Shadows of Rickey and Robinson: Bill Veeck, Larry Doby and the Advancement of Black Players in Baseball.* Ed. Peter M. Rutkoff. North Carolina: McFarland & Company, 2009.

Branson, Douglas M. *Greatness in the Shadows: Larry Doby and the Integration of the American League.* Lincoln: The University of Nebraska Press, 2016.

Cattau, Daniel. "So, Maybe There Really Such a Thing as 'The Natural'". *Smithsonian Magazine,* Vol. 22, Issue 4, July 1991.

Christensen, Lawrence O., William E. Foley, Gary R. Kremer, and Kenneth H. Winn. *Dictionary of Missouri Biography.* Columbia: University of Missouri Press, 1999.

Dickson, Paul. *Bill Veeck: Baseball's Greatest Maverick.* New York: Walker & Company, 2012.

Feller, Bob. *Now Pitching, Bob Feller: A Baseball Memoir.* New York: Citadel, 1990.

Freedman, Lew. *African American Pioneers of Baseball: A Biographical Encyclopedia.* Westport: Greenwood Publishing Company, 2007.

Gay, Timothy M., *Satch, Dizzy & Rapid Robert: The Wild Saga of Interracial Baseball Before Jackie Robinson.* New York: Simon and Schuster, 2010.

Green, Ben. *Spinning the Globe: The Rise, Fall, and Return to Greatness of the Harlem Globetrotters.* New York: Amistad, Reprint Edition, 2006

Heaphy, Leslie A. *The Negro Leagues 1869*-1960. North Carolina: McFarland & Company, 2003.

Hogan, Lawrence D. *Shades of Glory: The Negro Leagues and the Story of African American Baseball.* New York: National Geographic, 2006.

Holway, John B. *The Complete Book of Baseball's Negro Leagues: The Other Half of Baseball History.* Fern Park: Hastings House Publishers, 2001.

Lanctot, Neil. *Negro League Baseball: The Rise and Ruin of a Black Institution.* Philadelphia: University of Pennsylvania Press, 2004.

Lester Larry. *Rube Foster in his Own Time: On the Field and in the Papers with Black Baseball's Greatest Visionary.* North Carolina: McFarland & Company, 2012.

Lowry, Phillip J. *Green Cathedrals: The Ultimate Celebration of Major League and Negro League Ballparks.* New York: Walker Publishing Company, 2006.

Jacobson, Steve. *Carrying Jackie's Torch: The Players Who Integrated Baseball – and America.* Chicago: Lawrence Hill Books, 2007.

James, Bill. *The New Bill James Historical Baseball Abstract.* New York: Simon and Schuster, 1985.

Jolly, Kenneth S. *Black Liberation in the Midwest, The Struggle in St. Louis, Missouri, 1964-1970.* United Kingdom: Routledge, 2006.

Lebovitz, Hal. *The Best of Hal Lebovitz: Great Sportswriting from Six Decades in Cleveland.* Cleveland: Gray and Company Publishing, 2004.

Malloy, Jerry. *Sol White's History of Colored Base Ball, with Other Documents on the Early Black Game 1886-1936.* Lincoln: University of Nebraska Press, 1995.

Manelaro, Jim, and Scott Pitoniak. *Silver Seasons: The Story of the Rochester Red Wings.* Syracuse: Syracuse University Press, 1996.

McNeil, William F. *Black Baseball Out of Season: Pay for Play Outside the Negro Leagues.* Jefferson, McFarland and Company, 2007.

Moffi, Larry and Jonathan Kronstadt. *Crossing the Line: Black Major Leaguers 1947-1959.* Lincoln: The University of Nebraska Press, 2006.

Moore, Joseph Thomas. *Larry Doby: The Struggle of the American League's First Black Player.* New York, Dover Publications Inc., 2011

Nelson, Craig. *Pearl Harbor: From Infamy to Greatness.* New York: Simon and Schuster, 2016.

Nelson, Kevin. *The Golden Game: The Story of California Baseball.* Lincoln, The University of Nebraska Press, 2004.

O'Neil, Buck, David Conrads, and Steve Wulf. *I Was Right on Time: My Journey from the Negro Leagues to the Major Leagues.* New York: Simon and Schuster, Reprint Edition, 1997.

Odenkirk, James E. *Of Tribes and Tribulations: The Early Decades of the Cleveland Indians.* Jefferson, McFarland and Company, 2015.

Olson, Bruce R. *That St. Louis Thing, Vol 1: An American Story of Roots, Rhythm, and Race.* Lulu Publishing Services, 2016.

Russert, Tim. *Big Russ & Me: Father & Son: Lessons of Life.* New York: Hachette Books, 2014.

Paige, Satchel and David Lipman. *Maybe I'll Pitch Forever.* Lincoln: University of Nebraska Press, 1962.

Peterson, Robert. *Only the Ball was White: A history of Legendary Black Players and All-Black Professional Teams.* New York: Oxford University Press, 1970.

Pollack, Allan J. *Barnstormig to Heaven: Syd Pollack and his Great Black Teams.* Tuscaloosa: University of Alabama Press, 2006.

Revel, Dr. Layton. *Early Pioneers of the Negro Leagues: Charles Mills.* Center for Negro League Baseball Research, 2017

Revel, Dr. Layton. *Integration of Major League Baseball.* Center for Negro League Baseball Research.

Robinson, Frazier. *Catching Dreams: My Life in the Negro Baseball Leagues.* Syracuse: Syracuse University Press, 1999.

Rogosin, Donn. *Invisible Men: Life in Baseball's Negro Leagues.* Lincoln: Bison Books, 2007.

Simkus, Scott. *Outsider Baseball: The Weird World of Hardball on the Fringe, 1876-1950.* Chicago: Chicago Review Press, 2014.

Stone, Susan Michelle. *God's Will: Social Constructions of Health and Healing in the Mississippi Delta.* Berkeley: University of California, 1998.

Swaine, Rick. *Black Stars Who Made Baseball Whole.* North Carolina: McFarland & Company, 2005.

Swaine, Rick. *The Integration of Major League Baseball: A Team by Team History.* North Carolina: McFarland & Company, 2009.

Tygiel, Jules. *Baseball's Great Experiment: Jackie Robinson and his Legacy.* New York Random House, 1983.

Veeck, Bill with Ed Linn. *Veeck-As in Wreck*. New York: GP Putnam's Sons, 1962.

Wancho, Joseph, Rick Huhn, Leonard Levin, Bill Nowlin, and Steve Johnson. *Pitching to the Pennant: The 1954 Cleveland Indians*. Lincoln: The University of Nebraska Press, 2014.

Weintraub, Robert. *The Victory Season: The End of World War II and the Birth of Baseball's Golden Age*. New York: Little, Brown and Company, 2014.

White, Gaylon. *Singles and Smiles: How Artie Wilson Broke Baseball's Color Barrier*. Lanham: Rowman & Littlefield, 2018.

Yashinsky, Dan. *Tales for an Unknown City: Stories From One Thousand and One Friday Nights of Storytelling*. Quebec: McGill-Queen's University Press, 1990.

Zygner, Sam. *The Forgotten Marlins: A Tribute to the 1956-1960 Original Miami Marlins*. Lanham: The Scarecrow Press, 2013.

**Newspapers & Periodicals**

*The Akron Beacon Journal*

*Albuquerque Journal*

*Argus-Leader* (Sioux Falls, South Dakota)

*Atlanta Constitution*

*The Austin American* (Austin, Texas)

*The Bakersfield Californian* (Bakersfield, California)

*Baltimore Afro-American*

*Baseball Research Journal*

*The Baytown Sun* (Baytown, Texas)

*Beckley Post-Herald* (Beckley, West Virginia)

*Buffalo Courier-Express*

*Cincinnati Enquirer*

*Circleville Herald* (Circleville, Ohio)

*Clarion-Ledger* (Jackson, Mississippi)

*Cleveland Call and Post*

*Cleveland Indians Sketchbook*

*Cleveland News*

*Cleveland Plain Dealer*

*Collier's*

*The Coshocton Democrat* (Coshocton, Ohio)

*The Daily Courier* (Connellsville, Pennsylvania)

*Daily News* (New York, New York)

*Daily Press* (Newport News, Virginia)

*The Daily Times* (New Philadelphia, Ohio)

*The Daily Times* (Salisbury, Maryland)

*The Daily Tribune* (Wisconsin Rapids, Wisconsin)

*Dayton Daily News*

*The Dayton Herald*

*The Decatur Herald* (Decatur, Illinois)

*Delaware County Daily Times* (Swarthmore, Pennsylvania)

*Democrat and Chronicle* (Rochester, New York)

*Des Moines Tribune*

*Detroit Free Press*

*Elmira Advertiser* (Elmira, New York)

*The Evening Independent* (Massillon, Ohio)

*The Evening Sun* (Baltimore, Maryland)

*The Gazette* (Montreal, Canada)

*Honolulu Star-Bulletin*

*Indianapolis News*

*The Indianapolis Star*

*Jefferson City Post-Tribune* (Jefferson City, Missouri)

*Jet Magazine*

*Journal and Courier* (Lafayette, Indiana)

*The Journal Herald* (Dayton, Ohio)

*Kansas City Times* (Kansas City, Missouri)

*The Lethbridge Herald* (Lethbridge, Alberta, Canada)

*Logan Daily News* (Logan, Ohio)

*Long Beach Independent* (Long Beach, California)

*The Los Angeles Times*

*The Marion Star* (Marion, Ohio)

*Marysville Journal-Tribune* (Marysville, Ohio)

*The Mercury* (Pottstown, Pennsylvania)

*Miami News* (Miami, Florida)

*The Missoulian* (Missoula, Montana)

*Montana Standard* (Butte, Montana)

*The Morning News* (Wilmington, Delaware)

*Muncie Evening Press* (Muncie, Indiana)

*Newark Advocate* (Newark, Ohio)

*The News-Herald* (Franklin, Pennsylvania)

*The News-Messenger* (Fremont, Ohio)

*The News-Review* (Rosebud, Oregon)

*News-Journal* (Mansfield, Ohio)

*The News Tribune* (Fort Pierce, Florida)

*Oakland Tribune*

*The Ottawa Journal* (Ottawa, Ontario, Canada)

*The Paducah Sun* (Paducah, Kentucky)

*Palladium-Item* (Richmond, Indiana)

*Philadelphia Inquirer*

*Pittsburgh Courier*

*Pittsburgh Post-Gazette*

*Pittsburgh Press*

*The Post-Standard* (Syracuse, New York)

*Quad-City Times* (Davenport, Iowa)

*Rocky Mountain Telegram* (Rocky Mount, North Carolina)

*Rushville Republican* (Rushville, Indiana)

*The Salem News* (Salem, Ohio)

*The San Bernardino County Sun*

*Shamokin News-Dispatch* (Shamokin, Pennsylvania)

*The Sheboygan Press* (Sheboygan, Wisconsin)

*St. Cloud Times* (St. Cloud, Minnesota)

*St. Louis Post Dispatch*

*The St. Louis Star and Times*

*Sandusky Register* (Sandusky, Ohio)

*Smithsonian Magazine*

*The Sporting News*

*Star Tribune* (Minneapolis, Minnesota)

*Tampa Bay Times* (St. Petersburg, Florida)

*Tampa Tribune* (Tampa, Florida)

*The Terre Haute Tribune* (Terre Haute, Indiana)

*The Times-Recorder* (Zanesville, Ohio)

*The Tribune* (Coshocton, Ohio)

*Warren Times Mirror* (Warren, Pennsylvania)

*Washington C.H. Record-Herald* (Washington Court House, Ohio)

*Wilmington Daily Press Journal* (Wilmington, California)

*Wilmington News-Journal* (Wilmington, Ohio)

*Wisconsin State Journal* (Madison, Wisconsin)

**Website Articles**

Kopf, Dan. *The Great Migration: The African American Exodus from the South*. Published January 28, 2016. Accessed through http://priceonomics.com\

Murphy, Justin. *Luke Easter.* SABR (Society for American Baseball Research) Biography Project. Accessed through sabr.org/bioproject

Overfield, Joseph M. *Easter's Charisma, Remarkable Slugging Captivated Fans.* Published 1984. Accessed through Research.SABR.org.

Posnanski, Joe. *Invisible Man.* Accessed through http://NBCSports.com

**Other Websites**

http://Baseball-Almanac.com

http://BaseballHistoryDaily.com

http://BaseballReference.com

http://Census.gov

http://ClevelandHistorical.org

http://CNLBR.org

http://Collection.BaseballHall.org

http://eji.org/

http://milb.com

http://Research.SABR.org

http://Retrosheet.com

http://Sabr.org/bioproject

http://Wikipedia.com

# Index

## A

Aaron, Hank · viii
*Akron Beacon Journal* · ix, 14, - 75 -, - 88 -, - 92 -, - 96 -, - 98 -, - 109 -, - 112 -, - 150 -, - 155 -
Aluminum Ore Company · - 18 -
American Association · - 84 -, - 98 -, - 136 -
American League, The · vi, - 37 -, - 42 -, - 48 -, - 51 -, - 63 -, - 65 -, - 66 -, - 69 -, - 71 -, - 72 -, - 74 -, - 82 -, - 83 -, - 88 -, - 90 -, - 95 -, - 101 -, - 116 -, - 147 -
Artie Wilson · - 50 -, - 51 -, - 52 -, - 54 -, - 57 -, - 58 -, - 150 -
Askew, Jesse · - 25 -
Associated Press · - 102 -, - 107 -
Astaire, Fred · - 46 -
Averill, Earl · 15
Avila, Bobby · vi, - 87 -, - 88 -, - 89 -, - 92 -, - 96 -, - 116 -

## B

Babcock, Howard · - 78 -
Baker, Del · - 72 -
*Baltimore Elite Giants* · - 45 -, - 47 -, - 48 -
Baltimore Orioles · - 19 -
Bankhead, Dan · - 50 -
Bankhead, Sam · - 43 -, - 45 -, - 71 -
Banks, Ernie · viii
Bearden, Gene · - 73 -
Bell, 'Cool Papa' · - 20 -, - 25 -, - 30 -, - 33 -, - 37 -
Berardino, Johnny · - 66 -, - 73 -, - 80 -
Berra, Yogi · - 74 -

Birmingham Black Barons · - 30 -, - 31 -, - 34 -, - 48 -, - 49 -, - 52 -, - 84 -
Bisgeier, Harry · - 120 -, - 121 -
Blackball · - 20 -, - 21 -, - 22 -, - 23 -, - 24 -
Blatnik, Johnny · - 122 -
Bock, Wally · - 66 -, - 76 -, - 107 -
Boone, Ray · - 87 -, - 88 -, - 92 -, - 95 -, - 96 -
Boston Braves · 10, - 41 -, - 83 -
Boston Red Sox · - 63 -, - 69 -, - 78 -, - 91 -
Bottomley, Jim · - 19 -
Boudreau, Lou · 10, - 43 -, - 64 -, - 66 -, - 68 -, - 69 -, - 76 -, - 77 -, - 80 -, - 82 -, - 84 -, - 85 -, - 88 -, - 90 -
Brissie, Lou · v, - 96 -
Brooklyn Dodgers · 12, - 39 -, - 41 -, - 45 -, - 65 -, - 71 -
Brown, Willard · - 45 -, - 50 -
Buffalo Bisons · - 119 -, - 120 -, - 121 -, - 122 -, - 123 -, - 124 -, - 125 -, - 126 -, - 127 -, - 136 -
*Buffalo Courier-Express* · - 127 -, - 150 -

## C

Cain, Bob · - 134 -
Campanella, Roy · - 50 -, - 65 -
Case Western Reserve · 15
Cash, Ray · - 102 -
Cattau, Daniel J. · - 80 -, - 155 -
Cavraretta, Phil · - 122 -
Charleston Senators · - 117 -, - 136 -
Charleston, Oscar · - 20 -, - 37 -
Chicago American Giants · - 22 -, - 33 -, - 44 -

Chicago Cubs · - 77 -
Chicago White Sox · - 42 -, - 46 -, - 66 -, - 85 -, - 90 -, - 105 -, - 106 -
Chicago, Illinois · - 18 -, - 22 -, - 28 -, - 30 -, - 33 -, - 42 -, - 44 -, - 114 -, - 148 -, - 149 -
Cincinnati Crescents · - 30 -, - 31 -, - 32 -, - 33 -, - 34 -, - 35 -, - 51 -, - 53 -, - 59 -, - 60 -, - 71 -, - 82 -, - 136 -
Cincinnati Reds · - 28 -, - 31 -, - 84 -
Clark, Alfred 'Allie' · - 63 -, - 75 - 80
Cleveland Buckeyes · - 30 -, - 46 -
*Cleveland Call and Post* · - 54 -, - 150 -
Cleveland Indians · v, vi, ix, 10, - 27 -, - 41 -, - 45 -, - 51 -, - 54 -, - 59 -, - 62 -, - 64 -, - 68 -, - 69 -, - 70 -, - 76 -, - 86 -, - 89 -, - 90 -, - 91 -, - 92 -, - 95 -, - 102 -, - 107 -, - 113 -, - 114 -, - 129 -, - 130 -, - 136 -, - 148 -, - 150 -, - 151 -, - 155 -
Cleveland Municipal Stadium · 11, 13, 14, 15, - 69 -, - 81 -, - 97 -, - 109 -
*Cleveland Plain Dealer* · ix, - 65 -, - 68 -, - 69 -, - 78 -, - 79 -, - 92 -, - 97 -, - 100 -, - 105 -, - 109 -, - 134 -, - 137 -, - 151 -
Cleveland, Ohio · 10, - 52 -, - 54 -, - 62 -, - 63 -, - 65 -, - 71 -, - 72 -, - 76 -, - 84 -, - 85 -, - 93 -, - 94 -, - 99 -, - 100 -, - 102 -, - 103 -, - 105 -, - 110 -, - 118 -, - 122 -, - 129 -, - 130 -, - 133 -, - 134 -, - 136 -, - 148 -, - 150 -, - 151 -, - 155 -
Coahoma County, Mississippi · - 16 -, - 17 -
Cobbledick, Gordon · - 68 -, - 69 -, - 93 -, - 97 -

Colavito, Rocky · - 117 -, - 118 -
Columbus Jets · - 124 -
Colzie, Jim · - 44 -
Crosley Field · - 31 -, - 32 -, - 33 -
Cuban Stars · - 22 -

## D

Dandridge, Ray · - 84 -
Dayton Marcos · - 22 -
Dayton, Ohio · - 46 -, - 152 -
Dean, 'Dizzy' · - 19 -
*Delaware County Daily* · - 46 -, - 151 -
*Denver Post* Tournament · - 33 -
Detroit Stars · - 22 -
Detroit Tigers · 11, 13, - 78 -, - 88 -, - 91 -, - 120 -
DiMaggio, Joe · 15, - 34 -, - 83 -
Dixon, Bob · - 98 -
Doby, Larry · v, vii, - 40 -, - 42 -, - 43 -, - 45 -, - 49 -, - 50 -, - 52 -, - 54 -, - 57 -, - 63 -, - 65 -, - 67 -, - 73 -, - 74 -, - 77 -, - 78 -, - 79 -, - 87 -, - 89 -, - 90 -, - 93 -, - 95 -, - 147 -
Doerr, Bobby · - 82 -
Dropo, Walt · - 98 -

## E

Easter, J.C. · - 16 -, - 21 -, - 82 -
Easter, James · - 17 -, - 18 -, - 21 -, - 27 -
Easter, Maude · - 17 -
Easter, Vergil · vii, - 80 -, - 112 -, - 113 -, - 114 -, - 129 -, - 134 -
Easter, Wilbur · - 71 -
Easter. James · - 17 -

## F

Fain, Ferris · - 71 -, - 97 -
Feller, Bob · 13, - 27 -, - 67 -, - 71 -, - 73 -, - 76 -, - 87 -, - 90 -, - 91 -, - 131 -, - 147 -
Fields, Chinky · - 45 -
Fields, Wilmer · - 50 -
Finch, Frank · - 56 -, - 58 -, - 59 -
Fort Leonard Wood · - 27 -
Foster, Andrew 'Rube' · - 22 -
Foster, Andrew 'Rube' · - 22 -, - 23 -, - 24 -, - 148 -
Foxx, Jimmy · 15
Furillo, Carl · - 84 -

## G

Gaedel, Eddie · 10
Garcia, Mike · - 66 -, - 87 -, - 134 -
Garland, Judy · - 46 -
Gehrig, Lou · 15
Gibson, Josh · viii, - 36 -, - 37 -, - 38 -, - 39 -, - 40 -
Gillam, Jim · - 129 -
Glynn, Bill · - 109 -, - 111 -, - 116 -
Gordon, Joe · vi, - 43 -, - 66 -, - 77 -, - 79 -, - 80 -, - 88 -
Graham, Frank · - 28 -
Graham, Gordon · - 59 -
Grant, Frank · - 120 -
Great Migration, The · - 18 -
Greenberg, Hank · 11, 15, - 55 -, - 56 -, - 63 -, - 68 -, - 72 -, - 81 -, - 85 -, - 86 -, - 87 -, - 88 -, - 90 -, - 91 -, - 92 -, - 93 -, - 94 -, - 95 -, - 96 -, - 97 -, - 99 -, - 104 -, - 105 -, - 109 -, - 110 -
Greenwade, Tom · - 52 -
Griffith, Clark · - 37 -, - 38 -, - 40 -

## H

Hafey, Chick · - 19 -
Harlem Globetrotters · - 30 -, - 31 -, - 32 -, - 34 -, - 85 -, - 147 -
Harris, Bucky · - 56 -, - 57 -, - 68 -, - 72 -
Harris, Victor · - 45 -
Havana Sugar Kings · - 115 -
Haynes, Joe · 14
Hegan, Jim · v, - 43 -, - 77 -, - 87 -, - 89 -, - 95 -
Herrera, Frank · - 127 -
Hodges, Gil · - 98 -
Hogan, Lawrence · ix, - 49 -
Homestead Grays · 11, 12, - 36 -, - 37 -, - 38 -, - 39 -, - 40 -, - 41 -, - 43 -, - 44 -, - 45 -, - 46 -, - 47 -, - 48 -, - 49 -, - 51 -, - 55 -, - 82 -, - 124 -, - 136 -
Hornsby, Rogers · - 19 -
House of David · - 31 -, - 33 -
Hudson Field · - 46 -
Hutchinson, Fred · - 78 -

## I

Indianapolis ABCs · - 22 -
Indianapolis Clowns · - 44 -
Indianapolis Indians · - 84 -, - 98 -, - 99 -, - 116 -, - 117 -, - 136 -
International League · iv, - 112 -, - 114 -, - 119 -, - 120 -, - 122 -, - 123 -, - 126 -, - 127 -, - 136 -
Irvin, Monte · - 40 -, - 51 -, - 65 -, - 84 -

## J

Jackson, Rufus 'Sonnyman' · - 40 -
*Jefferson City Post-Tribune* · - 73 -, - 151 -

*Jet Magazine* · - 63 -, - 103 -, - 151 -
Jethroe, Sam 'The Jet' · - 25 -, - 26 -, - 83 -, - 93 -
Jim Crow Laws · - 16 -, - 18 -, - 61 -, - 111 -
Jonestown, Mississippi · - 16 -, - 17 -, - 26 -

## K

Kansas City Monarchs · - 22 -, - 25 -, - 33 -, - 40 -, - 45 -, - 55 -
Keltner, Ken · - 77 -
Kennedy, Bob · - 66 -, - 75 -, - 89 -
Kiner, Ralph · 15, - 73 -
Kramer, Jack · - 70 -
Kretlow, Lou · - 106 -
Kuzava, Bob · - 100 -, - 124 -

## L

Lafayette, Indiana · - 59 -, - 152 -
Landis, Kennesaw Mountain · - 55 -
Lemon, Bob · 13, - 76 -, - 78 -, - 87 -, - 89 -, - 106 -, - 134 -, - 137 -
Leonard, Buck · - 37 -, - 41 -, - 48 -
Liska, Ad · - 62 -
Litwhiler, Danny · - 84 -
Lopez, Al · - 84 -, - 87 -, - 92 -, - 95 -, - 96 -, - 98 -, - 107 -, - 109 -, - 111 -, - 138 -
*Los Angeles Times* · - 56 -, - 58 -, - 59 -, - 87 -, - 152 -

## M

Macon, Max · - 118 -
Maglie, Sal · - 111 -
Malamud, Bernard · vi
Manley, Effa · - 49 -, - 50 -
Manning, Gordon · - 82 -
Mantle, Mickey · - 131 -
Marquez, Luis · - 44 -, - 45 -, - 48 -, - 51 -
Mars, Billy · - 122 -
Martin, Billy · - 57 -
Matthews, Bob · - 128 -
Mayaguez Indians · - 50 -
Mays, Willie · viii, - 48 -, - 116 -
Mazer, Bill · - 123 -
McKechnie, Bill · - 43 -
Meusel, Bob · - 20 -
Miami Marlins · - 122 -, - 126 -, - 150 -
Mills, Charles 'Charlie' · - 20 -, - 23 -, - 24 -, - 149 -, - 154 -
Milwaukee Brewers · - 55 -
Minoso, Orestes 'Minnie' · - 48 -, - 54 -, - 60 -, - 89 -, - 90 -, - 106 -
Mitchell, Dale · 14, - 77 -, - 87 -, - 89 -
Mize, Johnny · - 108 -
Montreal Royals · - 41 -
Moryn, Walt · - 118 -
Musial, Stan · - 59 -, - 131 -

## N

National Association for the Advancement of Colored People (NAACP) · - 54 -
Negro American League · - 25 -, - 33 -, - 84 -
Negro League World Series · - 24 -, - 40 -, - 44 -, - 48 -
Negro League, The · ix, 11, 12, - 20 -, - 24 -, - 25 -, - 30 -, - 33 -, - 37 -, - 38 -, - 39 -, - 40 -, - 43 -, - 44 -, - 47 -, - 48 -, - 51 -, - 55 -, - 147 -, - 148 -, - 149 -, - 154 -
Negro National League · - 20 -, - 22 -, - 23 -, - 40 -, - 46 -, - 48 -, - 49 -, - 136 -

Nelson, Rocky · - 109 -, - 110 -, - 111 -, - 127 -
New Orleans Black Pelicans · - 34 -
New Orleans, Louisiana · - 31 -
New York Black Yankees · - 43 -, - 49 -
New York Cubans · - 47 -, - 48 -
New York Giants · - 51 -, - 65 -, - 75 -, - 84 -, - 88 -, - 116 -
New York Yankees · 13, - 51 -, - 57 -, - 63 -, - 71 -, - 74 -, - 86 -, - 92 -, - 100 -, - 102 -, - 105 -, - 107 -, - 116 -, - 124 -
Newark Bears · - 124 -
Newark Eagles · - 40 -, - 42 -, - 48 -, - 49 -, - 51 -, - 55 -
Newhouser, Hal · - 89 -
Nuxhall, Joe · - 28 -

# O

Offermann Stadium · - 121 -, - 124 -
Offermann, Frank · - 121 -
Oil City Refiners · - 46 -
O'Neil, Buck · 10, - 40 -, - 129 -
Ortiz, Lou · - 122 -
Ostrowki, Joe · - 101 -
Ottawa Athletics · - 112 -, - 114 -, - 115 -
Overfield, Joe · - 123 -, - 124 -, - 154 -
Owens, Jesse · - 34 -

# P

Pacific Coast League · - 53 -, - 55 -, - 56 -, - 58 -, - 59 -, - 60 -, - 61 -, - 62 -, - 63 -, - 88 -, - 121 -, - 136 -

Paige, Satchel · viii, - 22 -, - 33 -, - 36 -, - 37 -, - 40 -, - 50 -, - 51 -, - 54 -, - 65 -, - 112 -, - 126 -
*Palladium-Item (Richmond, Indiana)* · - 65 -, - 152 -
Parnell, Mel · - 107 -
Patriotas de Venezuela · - 44 -
Paul, Gabe · - 129 -, - 130 -
Pearl Harbor · - 26 -, - 27 -, - 148 -
Philadelphia Athletics · - 97 -
Philadelphia Phillies · - 20 -, - 41 -, - 54 -, - 83 -, - 127 -
Philadelphia Stars · - 88 -
Pieretti, Marino · - 67 -
*Pittsburgh Courier* · - 39 -, - 43 -, - 49 -, - 152 -
*Pittsburgh Post-Gazette* · - 39 -, - 73 -, - 153 -
*Plessy v. Ferguson* · - 16 -
Pollack, Syd · - 33 -, - 149 -
Polo Grounds · 12, - 47 -
Pope, Dave · - 95 -, - 99 -, - 100 -
Portland, Oregon · - 27 -
Posey, Cumberland 'Cum' · - 36 -, - 40 -
Puerto Rican Winter League · - 50 -, - 121 -, - 136 -

# R

Ray's Sausage · - 102 -
Reynolds, Allie · - 79 -
Richmond Virginians · - 126 -
Rickey, Branch · - 40 -, - 41 -, - 50 -, - 55 -, - 147 -
Ritchey, Johnny · - 55 -
Rizzuto, Phil · - 52 -, - 67 -
Robinson, Eddie · - 81 -, - 85 -
Robinson, Frazier 'Slow' · - 45 -, - 47 -
Robinson, Jackie · 12, - 39 -, - 41 -, - 42 -, - 49 -, - 50 -, - 65 -, - 93 -, - 109 -, - 147 -, - 149 -

Rochester Red Wings · - 122 -, - 127 -, - 128 -, - 129 -, - 134 -, - 136 -, - 148 -
Rosen, Al · vi, - 74 -, - 77 -, - 78 -, - 83 -, - 87 -, - 88 -, - 92 -, - 96 -, - 108 -, - 109 -, - 116 -, - 130 -, - 131 -, - 134 -
Ross, Bob · 13, 14
Rowland, Clarence · - 62 -
Russert, Tim · - 123 -, - 125 -, - 149 -
Ruth, Babe · vii, 15, - 36 -, - 39 -, - 48 -, - 73 -
Ryan, Ellis · - 71 -, - 84 -, - 92 -, - 97 -

## S

San Diego Padres · - 53 -, - 55 -, - 57 -, - 58 -, - 59 -, - 60 -, - 61 -, - 63 -, - 69 -, - 73 -, - 77 -, - 82 -, - 114 -, - 115 -, - 136 -
Sanford, Fred · - 79 -
Santa Rita Hotel (Tucson, Arizona) · - 74 -, - 95 -
Saperstein, Abe · iv, - 30 -, - 31 -, - 32 -, - 34 -, - 42 -, - 53 -, - 71 -, - 85 -
Schlemmer, Jim · ix, 15, - 75 -, - 89 -, - 96 -, - 109 -, - 111 -
Seattle Rainiers · - 56 -
Semproch, Ray · - 126 -
Serena, Bill · - 122 -
Simkus, Scott · viii, ix
Simpson, Harry 'Suitcase' · - 71 -, - 95 -
Simpson, Harry 'Suitcase' · - 88 -, - 90 -, - 100 -, - 137 -
Sisler, George · - 19 -
Smith, Quincy · - 30 -
Spahn, Warren · - 131 -
Sportsman's Park · - 19 -

St. Louis Browns · - 19 -, - 45 -, - 51 -, - 59 -, - 63 -, - 83 -, - 87 -, - 89 -, - 108 -, - 116 -
St. Louis Cardinals · - 19 -, - 20 -
St. Louis Stars · - 20 -, - 23 -, - 24 -, - 48 -, - 54 -, - 60 -, - 71 -, - 84 -, - 149 -, - 155 -
St. Louis Titanium Giants · iv, - 22 -, - 24 -, - 25 -, - 26 -, - 31 -, - 33 -, - 51 -
St. Louis, Missouri · - 16 -, - 17 -, - 18 -, - 19 -, - 20 -, - 21 -, - 22 -, - 23 -, - 24 -, - 25 -, - 26 -, - 27 -, - 28 -, - 29 -, - 30 -, - 43 -, - 45 -, - 56 -, - 61 -, - 63 -, - 71 -, - 76 -, - 108 -, - 148 -, - 149 -, - 153 -, - 155 -
Stanky, Eddie · - 41 -
Starr, Bill · - 55 -, - 58 -, - 60 -
Stengel, Casey · - 108 -, - 114 -
Stephens, Bryan · - 42 -
Stepin Fetchit · - 61 -
Stiglmeier, John C. · - 120 -, - 121 -
Suttles, Mule · - 20 -

## T

Tatum, Reese 'Goose' · - 34 -
Terre Haute, Indiana · - 44 -, - 153 -
*The Daily Times (New Phildelphia, Ohio)* · - 80 -, - 97 -, - 151 -
*The Dayton Herald* · - 46 -, - 151 -
*The Evening Independent (Massilon, Ohio)* · - 98 -, - 151 -
The Great Depression · - 21 -
*The Salem News (Salem, Ohio)* · - 81 -, - 153 -
*The Sporting News* · - 19 -, - 35 -, - 55 -, - 57 -, - 59 -, - 61 -, - 80 -, - 102 -, - 153 -

The Titanium Pigment Company · - 24 -
Thompson Ramo Woolridge (TRW) · - 129 -, - 131 -, - 132 -, - 133 -, - 134 -
Thompson, Hank · - 45 -, - 51 -, - 65 -, - 84 -
Thurman, Bob · 12, - 44 -, - 45 -, - 124 -
Thurston, Hollis · - 55 -, - 56 -
Toronto Maple Leafs · - 123 -, - 126 -
Tris Speaker · - 71 -, - 95 -
Trosky, Hal · 15
Trouppe, Quincy · - 95 -
Tucker, Thurman · - 73 -
Tucson, Arizona · - 73 -, - 74 -, - 75 -, - 95 -, - 111 -
Tygiel, Jules · ix, - 61 -, - 149 -

# V

Veeck, Bill · 10, 11, 12, - 41 -, - 42 -, - 43 -, - 51 -, - 52 -, - 53 -, - 54 -, - 55 -, - 59 -, - 63 -, - 71 -, - 72 -, - 93 -, - 134 -, - 147 -, - 149 -, - 155 -
Vernon, Mickey · - 68 -, - 70 -, - 72 -, - 75 -, - 77 -, - 79 -, - 80 -, - 81 -, - 84 -, - 109 -
Vollmer, Clyde · - 117 -, - 121 -

# W

Washington Senators · 13, - 37 -, - 38 -, - 81 -, - 83 -, - 90 -, - 101 -
Weiss, George · - 51 -, - 52 -
Welch, Winfield · - 34 -, - 71 -
Wells, Willie · - 20 -, - 37 -
Wertz, Vic · - 116 -
West, Max · - 60 -, - 62 -
Westrum, Wes · - 75 -
White, Annie · - 18 -
Wilkinson, J.L. · - 25 -
Williams, Ted · 15, - 59 -, - 69 -, - 70 -, - 81 -
Willis, Chester and Lucille · - 74 -, - 95 -
*Wilmington Daily Press Journal* · - 80 -, - 153 -
Wolf, Al · - 59 -, - 63 -, - 87 -
World War II · vi, - 17 -, - 26 -, - 34 -, - 76 -, - 150 -
Wynn, Early · - 76 -, - 81 -, - 87 -, - 137 -, - 138 -

# Y

Yankee Stadium · - 37 -, - 47 -, - 100 -
Young, A.S. 'Doc' · - 63 -
Young, Eddie 'Pepper' · - 33 -, - 44 -

# Z

Zoldak, Sam · - 66 -, - 86 -

**Introduction: 'A Prodigious Swat'**

[1] Veeck, Bill with Ed Linn. *Veeck-As in Wreck* (New York: GP Putnam's Sons, 1962), Pg. 114
[2] *Detroit Free Press*, November 22, 1949
[3] All box scores, standings, statistics, and lineups accessed through BaseballReference.com
[4] Swaine, Rick. *Black Stars Who Made Baseball Whole*. (North Carolina: McFarland & Company, 2005), Pg. 77
[5] Wancho, Joseph, Rick Huhn, Leonard Levin, Bill Nowlin, and Steve Johnson. *Pitching to the Pennant: The 1954 Cleveland Indians.* (Lincoln: The University of Nebraska Press, 2014), Pg. 181
[6] Cattau, Daniel. St. Louis Post Dispatch. 1992 April 5, Pg. 8
[7] BaseballReference.com
[8] BaseballReference.com
[9] *News-Journal (Mansfield, OH)*, June 24, 1950
[10] Ibid.
[11] *Akron Beacon Journal*, June 24, 1950
[12] Ibid.
[13] Posanski, Joe. *Invisible Man*. Accessed through NBCSports.com

**'From the Delta to the Gateway City' Notes**

[1] Cattau, 10
[2] Author's personal collection
[3] Cattau, 8
[4] Census data accessed through http://www.census.gov
[5] Stone, Susan Michelle. *God's Will: Social Constructions of Health and Healing in the Mississippi Delta* (Berkeley: University of California, 1998), Pgs. 19-20
[6] Census data
[7] Data provided by the Equal Justice Initiative report 'Lynching in America: Confronting the Legacy of Racial Terror' accessed through https://eji.org/
[8] Cattau, 10
[9] Ibid.
[10] Ibid.
[11] Kopf, Dan. *The Great Migration: The African American Exodus from The South*. Published January 28, 2016. Accessed through http://priceonomics.com
[12] Census data accessed through http://www.census.gov
[13] Cattau, 10
[14] Jolly, Kenneth S. *Black Liberation in the Midwest, The Struggle in St. Louis, Missouri, 1964-1970* (United Kingdom: Routledge, 2006), Pgs. 6-7
[15] Olson, Bruce R. *That St. Louis Thing, Vol 1: An American Story of Roots, Rhythm, and Race.* (Lulu Publishing Services, 2016), Pgs. 342-343
[16] Statistics, lineups accessed through BaseballReference.com
[17] Cattau, 10
[18] Ibid.
[19] Peterson, Robert. *Only the Ball was White: A history of Legendary Black Players and All-Black Professional Teams*. (New York: Oxford University Press,

1970), Pg. 3
[20] Hogan, Lawrence D. *Shades of Glory: The Negro Leagues and the Story of African American Baseball* (National Geographic, 2006), Pg. 135
[21] Gay, Timothy M., *Satch, Dizzy & Rapid Robert: The Wild Saga of Interracial Baseball Before Jackie Robinson* (New York: Simon and Schuster, 2010), Pg. 29
[22] Simkus, Scott. Outsider Baseball: The Weird World of Hardball on the Fringe, 1876-1950 (Chicago: Chicago Review Press, 2014), Pg. 266
[23] James, Bill. *The New Bill James Historical Baseball Abstract.* (New York: Simon and Schuster, 1985), Pg. 178
[24] Lowry, Phillip J. *Green Cathedrals: The Ultimate Celebration of Major League and Negro League Ballparks* (New York: Walker Publishing Company, 2006), Pg. 203
[25] Playoff results courtesy of the Center for Negro League Baseball Research, accessed through cnlbr.org
[26] Swaine, 77

**'The Titanium Giants and the Wartime Years' Notes**

[1] Heaphy, Leslie A. *The Negro Leagues 1869-1960* (McFarland & Company, North Carolina, 2003), Pgs. 40-43
[2] Malloy, Jerry. *Sol White's History of Colored Base Ball, with Other Documents on the Early Black Game 1886-1936.* (Lincoln: University of Nebraska Press, 1995), Pg. 152
[3] Malloy, xxiv
[4] Lester Larry. *Rube Foster in his Own Time: On the Field and in the Papers with Black Baseball's Greatest Visionary* (North Carolina: McFarland & Company, 2012), Pg. 169
[5] Hogan, 249
[6] Ibid.
[7] Revel, Layton. *Early Pioneers of the Negro Leagues: Charles Mills* (Center for Negro League Baseball Research, 2017), Pg. 38
[8] Author's note: his tenure in beginning with the S. Louis Titanium Giants has been listed by several authors as 1937, though recent research has pointed to 1935 as the more accurate year, including from the Center for Negro League Baseball Research.
[9] Swaine, 78
[10] Cattau, 10
[11] Ibid.
[12] Posanski
[13] *The St. Louis Star and Times,* August 12, 1949
[14] Quoted in Jethroe's obituary, written by Mike Carlson for *The Guardian* on July 16, 2001.
[15] Christensen, Lawrence O., William E. Foley, Gary R. Kremer, and Kenneth H. Winn. *Dictionary of Missouri Biography* (Columbia: University of Missouri Press, 1999), Pg. 269
[16] Nelson, Craig. *Pearl Harbor: From Infamy to Greatness* (New York: Simon and Schuster, 2016), Pg. 345

[17] Feller, Bob. *Now Pitching, Bob Feller: A Baseball Memoir* (New York: Citadel, 1990), Pg. 116
[18] Simkus, 256
[19] Cattau, 11
[20] Weintraub, Robert. *The Victory Season: The End of World War II and the Birth of Baseball's Golden Age* (New York: Little, Brown and Company, 2014), Pg. 6
[21] O'Neil, Buck, David Conrads, and Steve Wulf. *I Was Right on Time: My Journey from the Negro Leagues to the Major Leagues* (New York: Simon and Schuster, Reprint Edition, 1997), Pg. 51
[22] Swaine, 78
[23] Moffi, Larry and Jonathan Kronstadt. *Crossing the Line: Black Major Leaguers 1947-1959.* (Lincoln: The University of Nebraska Press, 2006), Pg. 38

**'Abe Saperstein and the Crescents' Notes**

[1] Manning, Gordon. *They're Gonna Like Big Luke*. Colliers Magazine, August 5, 1950. Pg. 70
[2] BaseballReference.com
[3] Manning, 70
[4] Green, Ben. *Spinning the Globe: The Rise, Fall, and Return to Greatness of the Harlem Globetrotters* (New York: Amistad, Reprint Edition, 2006), Pg. 7
[5] Manning, 70
[6] *Cincinnati Enquirer*, March 26, 1946
[7] Manning, 70
[8] *Cincinnati Enquirer*, July 24, 1946
[9] *Cincinnati Enquirer*, July 30, 1946
[10] *Cincinnati Enquirer*, July 31, 1946
[11] *Cincinnati Enquirer*, August 16, 1946
[12] Rogosin, Donn. *Invisible Men: Life in Baseball's Negro Leagues* (Lincoln: Bison Books, 2007), Pgs. 136-137
[13] Heaphy, 148
[14] Pollack, Allan J. *Barnstormig to Heaven: Syd Pollack and his Great Black Teams* (Tuscaloosa: University of Alabama Press, 2006), Pgs. 100-102
[15] *Honolulu Star-Bulletin,* September 21, 1946
[16] Manning, 70
[17] *Honolulu Star-Bulletin,* September 27, 1946
[18] Robinson, Frazier. *Catching Dreams: My Life in the Negro Baseball Leagues* (Syracuse: Syracuse University Press, 1999), Pgs. 178-79
[19] O'Neil, 63
[20] *The Sporting News*, March 30, 1949
[21] Manning, 70.
[22] Swaine, 86

**'1947: An Heir Apparent Arises, the Color Barrier Falls' Notes**

[1] Yashinsky, Dan. *Tales for an Unknown City: Stories From One Thousand and One Friday Nights of Storytelling* (Quebec: McGill-Queen's University Press, 1990) Pgs. 124-25
[2] This is ascertained through the author's personal research.
[3] Freedman, Lew. *African American Pioneers of Baseball: A Biographical Encyclopedia* (Westport: Greenwood Publishing Company, 2007) Pg. 55
[4] Ibid.
[5] *Sporting News, June 3, 1938*
[6] Lowry, 236
[7] Ibid., 58
[8] Statistics and season results accessed through BaseballReference.com
[9] *Baltimore Afro-American*, June 3, 1944
[10] Freeman, 63
[11] Tygiel, Jules. *Baseball's Great Experiment: Jackie Robinson and his Legacy* (New York: Random House, 1983), Pg. 40
[12] Freeman, 59
[13] Freeman, 64
[14] *Pittsburgh Post-Gazette*, January 21, 1947
[15] Tygiel, 71
[16] Revel, Dr. Layton, *Integration of Major League Baseball*. Accessed through CNLBR.org, pgs. 7-8
[17] Paige, Satchel and David Lipman. *Maybe I'll Pitch Forever.* (Lincoln: University of Nebraska Press, 1962), Pgs.xiii-xiv
[18] Revel, 10
[19] Statistics, rosters, game results accessed through BaseballReference.com
[20] Cattau, 11
[21] Tygiel, 178
[22] BaseballReference.com
[23] Tygiel, 184-85
[24] BaseballReference.com
[25] Robinson, 121
[26] Swaine, Rick. *The Integration of Major League Baseball: A Team by Team History* (North Carolina: McFarland & Company, 2009), Pg. 49
[27] BaseballReference.com
[28] Revel, 13
[29] Jacobson, Steve. *Carrying Jackie's Torch: The Players Who Integrated Baseball – and America* (Chicago: Lawrence Hill Books, 2007), Pgs. 31-32
[30] Veeck, 170
[31] Appearance log accessed through BaseballReference.com
[32] *Pittsburgh Courier,* May 3, 1947
[33] *Philadelphia Inquirer,* May 19, 1947
[34] *The Morning News* (Wilmington, Delaware), June 7, 1947
[35] Pollack, 123
[36] Manning, 70
[37] Ibid.

[38] Author's Note: There is not solid evidence of the marriage of Easter and Bethune, outside the feature story in Collier's. It is clear that it couldn't have lasted long, he bought a home in Cleveland with his wife Vergil Lowe, a Cleveland native, in the 'early 1950's'. Vergil and Luke were married until his death.
[39] Posanski, NBCSports.com

**'The Negro Leagues' Notes**

[1] Robinson, 122
[2] Swaine, 4
[3] Player's past team histories accessed through BaseballReference.com
[4] *Pittsburgh Courier*, March 20, 1948
[5] *Pittsburgh Post-Gazette*, April 29, 1948
[6] *The Journal Herald* (Dayton, Ohio), April 28, 1948
[7] *The Pittsburgh Press*, April 29, 1948
[8] *The News-Herald* (Franklin, Pennsylvania), May 5, 1948
[9] *The Daily Courier* (Connellsville, Pennsylvania), May 6, 1948
[10] *Pittsburgh Post-Gazette*, May 31, 1948
[11] *The Dayton Herald*, July 23, 1948
[12] *Delaware County Daily Times*, July 22, 1948
[13] Author's Note: You may remember this home run being alluded to way back in the Introduction.
[14] Robinson, 119
[15] Transactions accessed through BaseballReference.com
[16] Ibid.
[17] Image of the poster available through the Baseball Hall of Fame's archives. Accessed through collection.baseballhall.org
[18] Ibid.
[19] *St. Louis Post Dispatch*, August 25, 1948
[20] Negro League standings accessed through BaseballReference.com
[21] Holway, John B. *The Complete Book of Baseball's Negro Leagues: The Other Half of Baseball History* (Fern Park: Hastings House Publishers, 2001), Pgs. 459-60
[22] Ibid.
[23] Manning, 70
[24] Hogan, 349
[25] Lanctot, Neil. *Negro League Baseball: The Rise and Ruin of a Black Institution* (Philadelphia: University of Pennsylvania Press, 2004), Pg. 338
[26] *Demise of the Negro Leagues* accessed through CNLBR.Org
[27] Ibid.
[28] Swaine, 4
[29] Statistics accessed through BaseballReference.com
[30] Lanctot, 338
[31] *Tampa Bay Times* (St. Petersburg, Florida), January 25, 1949
[32] Murphy, Justin. SABR (Society for American Baseball Research) Biography

Project, Luke Easter. Accessed through sabr.org/bioproject
[33] Transaction accessed through BaseballReference.com
[34] *Pittsburgh Post-Gazette*, February 26, 1949
[35] *Cleveland News*, February 10, 1949
[36] Lanctot, 347-54
[37] White, Gaylon. *Singles and Smiles: How Artie Wilson Broke Baseball's Color Barrier*. (Lanham: Rowman & Littlefield, 2018), Pgs. 45-46
[38] Manning, 70

**'The Coastal Phenom' Notes**

[1] Zingg, Paul J. and Mark D. Medeiros. *Runs, Hits, and an Era: The Pacific Coast League, 1903-58.* (Chicago: University of Illinois Press, 2004)
[2] *Cleveland Call and Post,* February 1949
[3] Dickson, Paul. *Bill Veeck: Baseball's Greatest Maverick.* (New York: Walker & Company, 2012), Pg. 173
[4] Jacobson, 36
[5] Beck, Peggy. *Working in the Shadows of Rickey and Robinson: Bill Veeck, Larry Doby and the Advancement of Black Players in Baseball.* Ed. Peter M. Rutkoff ((North Carolina: McFarland & Company, 2009), Pg. 110
[6] Cattau, 12
[7] Swaine, 77
[8] Manning, 70
[9] *The Los Angeles Times*, March 6, 1949
[10] *The Los Angeles Times*, March 9, 1949
[11] *The News-Review (Rosebud, Oregon),* March 11, 1949
[12] *Oakland Tribune,* March 13, 1949
[13] *The Los Angeles Times*, March 20, 1949
[14] Nelson, Kevin. *The Golden Game: The Story of California Baseball.* (Lincoln, The University of Nebraska Press, 2004), Pg. 261
[15] *The Sporting News,* March 30, 1949
[16] White, 12
[17] *The Akron Beacon Journal*, March 29, 1949
[18] *The Akron Beacon Journal*, March 30, 1949
[19] *The Los Angeles Times*, March 31, 1949
[20] Ibid.
[21] Montana Standard (Butte, Montana), April 5, 1949
[22] Cattau, Daniel. "So, Maybe There Really Such a Thing as 'The Natural'". *Smithsonian Magazine,* Vol. 22, Issue 4, July 1991.
[23] *The Sporting News,* March 30, 1949
[24] *The Los Angeles Times,* May 28, 1949
[25] *Journal and Courier,* April 6, 1949
[26] *Oakland Tribune,* April 6, 1949
[27] White, 66
[28] *The Los Angeles Times,* May 31, 1949
[29] *The Los Angeles Times,* May 28, 1949

[30] Tygiel, 252
[31] *The Sporting News,* June 22, 1949
[32] *Akron Beacon Journal,* May 25, 1949
[33] *The Sporting News,* May 4, April 27, 1949
[34] Author's Note: Even in reviewing the box scores, it's hard to pinpoint the exact date of the beaning. The date range is a best estimation based on when he went to get the knee looked at by medical.
[35] *The Los Angeles Times,* July 1, 1949
[36] Statistics accessed through BaseballReference.com
[37] Moffi, 38
[38] White, 65
[39] Hogan, 361
[40] *The Los Angeles Times,* August 10, 1949
[41] Statistics accessed through BaseballReference.com
[42] *The Los Angeles Times,* August 11, 1949
[43] *The Sandusky Register,* August 12, 1949

**'A (Bitter) Cup of Coffee' Notes**

[1] *Palladium-Item* (Richmond, Indiana), December 30, 1949
[2] Cattau, 12
[3] *Cleveland Plain Dealer,* August 12, 1949
[4] *Cleveland Plain Dealer,* August 1, 1949
[5] Manning, 70
[6] Lebovitz, Hal. *The Best of Hal Lebovitz: Great Sportswriting from Six Decades in Cleveland.* (Cleveland: Gray and Company Publishing, 2004) Pg. 67
[7] Statistics and box scores accessed through BaseballReference.com
[8] Ibid.
[9] *Cleveland Plain Dealer,* August 13, 1947
[10] Author's Note: The *Plain Dealer* noted that Appling, who was playing shortstop that day, fielded Easter's ground ball. BaseballReference.com records it went to the third baseman.
[11] *Cleveland Plain Dealer,* August 26, 1949
[12] *Cleveland Plain Dealer,* August 30, 1949
[13] Ibid.
[14] *Cleveland Plain Dealer,* September 3, 1949
[15] Manning, 71
[16] Box score and play-by-play accessed through BaseballReference.com
[17] *Cleveland Plain Dealer,* September 22, 1949
[18] Manning, 71
[19] Standings and statistics accessed through BaseballReference.com
[20] Cattau, 12
[21] *Los Angeles Times,* October 25, 1949
[22] Gay, 273
[23] *Los Angeles Times,* October 25, 1949
[24] *The Akron Beacon Journal,* November 18, 1949
[25] *The Pittsburgh Courier,* December 31, 1949

[26] *The Mercury* (Pottstown, Pennsylvania), November 23, 1949
[27] Manning, 71
[28] *News-Journal* (Mansfield, Ohio), January 15, 1950
[29] *The Pittsburgh Courier*, December 31, 1949

**'Breakout' Notes**

[1] Posnanski, accessed through NBCSports.com
[2] *Pittsburgh Post-Gazette,* February 2, 1950
[3] *Jefferson City Post-Tribune,* February 2, 1950
[4] Manning, 71
[5] Moffi, 39
[6] White, 51
[7] Odenkirk, James E. *Of Tribes and Tribulations: The Early Decades of the Cleveland Indians* (Jefferson, McFarland and Company, 2015), Pg. 238
[8] Branson, Douglas M. *Greatness in the Shadows: Larry Doby and the Integration of the American League.* (Lincoln, University of Nebraska Press, 2016), Pg. 195
[9] *Cleveland Plain Dealer*, March 25, 1956
[10] Moore, Joseph Thomas. *Larry Doby: The Struggle of the American League's First Black Player. (*New York, Dover Publications Inc., 2011), Pg. 93
[11] *Albuquerque Journal,* April 2, 1950
[12] *The Marion Star (*Marion, Ohio), April 1, 1950
[13] *Akron Beacon Journal,* April 10, 1950
[14] Odenkirk, 247
[15] Odenkirk, 251
[16] Lebovitz, 68
[17] Opening Day lineup accessed through BaseballReference.com
[18] *News-Journal* (Mansfield, Ohio), April 18, 1950.
[19] *Cleveland Plain Dealer*, April 19, 1950
[20] *Cleveland Plain Dealer*, May 5, 1950
[21] Statistics and schedule accessed through BaseballReference.com
[22] *Cleveland Plain Dealer*, May 7, 1950
[23] Ibid.
[24] *Dayton Daily News,* May 9, 1950
[25] *The Daily Times* (New Philadelphia, Ohio), June 2, 1950
[26] *Akron Beacon Journal*, June 2, 1950
[27] *Sporting News,* May
[28] *The Daily Times* (New Philadelphia, Ohio), June 6, 1950
[29] *Wilmington Daily Press Journal* (Wilmington, California), November 29, 1950
[30] Cattau, 12
[31] Statistics accessed through BaseballReference.com
[32] *The Salem News* (Salem, Ohio), June 20, 1950
[33] Transactions accessed through BaseballReference.com
[34] Statistics accessed through BaseballReference.com
[35] Manning, 20

[36] Ibid., 21, 70
[37] Cattau, 8
[38] Manning, 70
[39] Standings accessed through BaseballReference.com
[40] Ibid.
[41] Ibid.
[42] *Daily Press* (Newport News, Virginia), October 10, 1950
[43] Ibid.
[44] Ibid, October 11, 1950
[45] Elmira Advertiser (Elmira, New York), October 10, 1950
[46] *The Baytown Sun* (Baytown, Texas), October 23, 1950
[47] *Tampa Bay Times* (St. Petersburg, Florida), November 6, 1950
[48] *The Evening Sun* (Baltimore, Maryland), November 10, 1950
[49] Ibid.
[50] *Pittsburgh Courier*, November 18, 1950
[51] News-Journal (Mansfield, Ohio), December 24, 1950

**'Still Chasin' the Yankees' Notes**

[1] *News-Journal* (Mansfield, Ohio), July 20, 1951
[2] *Rocky Mountain Telegram* (Rocky Mount, North Carolina), January 3, 1951.
[3] *Cleveland Plain Dealer,* February 27, 1951
[4] *News-Journal* (Mansfield, Ohio), July 20, 1951
[5] *The Salem News* (Salem, Ohio), March 5, 1951
[6] *Los Angeles Times,* March 17, 1951
[7] *Quad-City Times* (Davenport, Iowa), March 28, 1951
[8] Statistics accessed through BaseballReference.com
[9] Cleveland Indians Sketchbook, 1951
[10] *The Daily Tribune* (Wisconsin Rapids, Wisconsin), October 6, 1950
[11] *Akron Beacon Journal,* April 8, 1951
[12] Opening Day lineup accessed through BaseballReference.com
[13] *The Daily Times* (New Philadelphia, Ohio), April 18, 1951
[14] *Akron Beacon Journal,* April 29, 1951
[15] Odenkirk, 253
[16] Statistics accessed through BaseballReference.com
[17] Ibid.
[18] Ibid.
[19] *The News-Messenger* (Fremont, Ohio), August 23, 1951
[20] Schedules accessed through BaseballReference.com
[21] *Akron Beacon Journal,* October 14, 1951
[22] Odenkirk, 255
[23] *Akron Beacon Journal,* October 16, 1951
[24] *Akron Beacon Journal,* November 8, 1951
[25] *Cleveland Plain Dealer*, November 21, 1951
[26] *The Evening Independent* (Massillon, Ohio), December 20, 1951

**'Well, I'll be Damned' Notes**

[1] Cattau, 12
[2] *Akron Beacon Journal,* February 19, 1952
[3] *Circleville Herald* (Circleville, Ohio), February 2, 1952
[4] *Akron Beacon Journal,* February 20, 1952
[5] *Akron Beacon Journal,* April 11, 1952
[6] *Circleville Herald* (Circleville, Ohio), April 11, 1952
[7] *Akron Beacon Journal,* April 11, 1952
[8] *Akron Beacon Journal,* February 20, 1952
[9] *Marysville Journal-Tribune* (Marysville, Ohio), June 2, 1952
[10] *The Daily Times* (New Philadelphia, Ohio), June 4, 1952
[11] *Cleveland Plain Dealer,* June 1, 1952
[12] Cattau, Daniel. "So, Maybe There Really Such a Thing as 'The Natural'". *Smithsonian Magazine,* Vol. 22, Issue 4, July 1991.
[13] *Cleveland Plain Dealer,* June 6, 1952
[14] Ibid.
[15] *The Evening Independent* (Massillon, Ohio), June 3, 1952
[16] *Akron Beacon Journal,* June 16, 1952
[17] *Chillicothe Gazette,* July 1, 1952
[18] Ibid.
[19] Simkus, 259
[20] *The Indianapolis News,* July 2, 1952
[21] *Indianapolis Star* July 4, 1952
[22] *Indianapolis Star* July 5, 1952
[23] Statistics accessed from BaseballReference.com
[24] *The Terre Haute Tribune,* July 6, 1952
[25] *Rushville Republican,* July 14, 1952
[26] *Cleveland Plain Dealer,* July 9, 1952
[27] *Cleveland Plain Dealer,* July 11, 1952
[28] *Palladium-Item* (Richmond, Indiana), July 15, 1952
[29] Simkus, 261
[30] *The Salem News* (Salem, Ohio), July 16, 1952
[31] *Cleveland Plain Dealer,* July 16, 1952
[32] *Akron Beacon Journal,* July 28, 1952
[33] *Cleveland Plain Dealer,* July 28, 1952
[34] *The Evening Independent* (Massillon, Ohio), August 1, 1952
[35] *The Evening Independent* (Massillon, Ohio), August 21, 1952
[36] *The Marion Star* (Marion, Ohio), September 11, 1952
[37] Statistics and records accessed through BaseballReference.com
[38] Ibid.
[39] Annual award winners accessed through Baseball-Almanac.com
[40] *The Sandusky Register* (Sandusky, Ohio), October 23, 1952
[41] *Akron Beacon Journal,* August 13, 1953
[42] Information obtained through a write-up on BaseballHistoryDaily.com
[43] *The Sandusky Register* (Sandusky, Ohio), October 23, 1952
[44] *Muncie Evening Press* (Muncie, Indiana), December 25, 1952
[45] Posnanski, accessed through NBCSports.com
[46] *Akron Beacon Journal,* February 9, 1953

### 'On the Outs' Notes

[1] *The Times Recorder* (Zanesville, Ohio) April 14, 1953
[2] Author's Note: The Daniel Jack story compiled between Scott Simkus' *Outsider Baseball: The Weird World of Hardball on the Fringe, 1876-1950*, Pgs. 261-62, as well as the *Cleveland Plain Dealer* articles from April 12 and April 13.
[3] *The Journal Herald* (Dayton, Ohio) April 15, 1953
[4] Simkus, 262
[5] Ibid.
[6] *The Tribune* (Coshocton, Ohio), April 19, 1953
[7] Lebovitz, 67
[8] *Logan Daily News (*Logan, Ohio), April 20, 1953
[9] Statistics accessed through BaseballReference.com
[10] *Des Moines Tribune*, August 8, 1953
[11] Ibid.
[12] Statistics accessed through BaseballReference.com
[13] Ibid.
[14] *The Journal Herald* (Dayton, Ohio), September 15, 1953
[15] Statistics accessed through BaseballReference.com
[16] Ibid.
[17] *Akron Beacon Journal,* October 2, 1953
[18] Swaine, 81
[19] *Cleveland Plain Dealer,* November 18, 1953
[20] *Cleveland Plain Dealer,* November 19, 1953
[21] Majestic Hotel description accessed through ClevelandHistorical.org
[22] *The Tribune* (Coshocton, Ohio), December 12, 1953
[23] *The Times Recorder* (Zanesville, Ohio), March 10, 1954
[24] *The Times Recorder* (Zanesville, Ohio), March 16, 1954
[25] Ibid.
[26] *Akron Beacon Journal,* April 5, 1954
[27] *Washington C.H. Record-Herald* (Washington Court House, Ohio), April 13, 1954
[28] *Wilmington News-Journal* (Wilmington, Ohio), May 13, 1954
[29] *Akron Beacon Journal,* May 13, 1954
[30] Cattau, 12

### 'What Next' Notes

[1] *The San Bernardino County Sun*, March 10, 1955
[2] *The Ottawa Journal* (Ottawa, Ontario, Canada), May 18, 1954
[3] Ibid.
[4] Ibid.
[5] *The Ottawa Journal* (Ottawa, Ontario, Canada), May 19, 1954
[6] *The Lethbridge Herald* (Lethbridge, Alberta, Canada), June 4, 1954
[7] *The Ottawa Journal* (Ottawa, Ontario, Canada), June 25, 1954

[8] *The Ottawa Journal* (Ottawa, Ontario, Canada), July 15, 1954
[9] Statistics accessed through BaseballReference.com
[10] *Long Beach Independent* (Long Beach, California), July 19, 1954.
[11] *The San Bernardino County Sun*, August 9, 1954
[12] Lineups and statistics accessed through BaseballReference.com
[13] *Tampa Tribune* (Tampa, Florida), October 8, 1954
[14] *Kansas City Times* (Kansas City, Missouri), October 14, 1954
[15] *The Cincinnati Enquirer*, November 21, 1954
[16] *Oakland Tribune*, December 24, 1954
[17] Murphy
[18] *Beckley Post-Herald* (Beckley, West Virginia), January 9, 1955
[19] *The News Tribune* (Fort Pierce, Florida), March 20, 1955
[20] *St. Cloud Times* (St. Cloud, Minnesota), April 20, 1955
[21] *Argus-Leader* (Sioux Falls, South Dakota), April 22, 1955
[22] *The Indianapolis Star*, April 26, 1955
[23] *Wisconsin State Journal* (Madison, Wisconsin), April 23, 1955
[24] *Pittsburgh Courier*, May 7, 1955
[25] *Star Tribune* (Minneapolis, Minnesota), June 26, 1955
[26] *The Bakersfield Californian* (Bakersfield, California), June 29, 1955
[27] *Muncie Evening Press (Muncie, Indiana)*, August 9, 1955
[28] *Des Moines Tribune* (Des Moines, Iowa), August 18, 1955
[29] Statistics accessed through BaseballReference.com
[30] *Decatur Herald* (Decatur, Illinois), October 20, 1955

**'International League Royalty' Notes**

[1] *Indianapolis Star*, October 30, 1955
[2] *Sandusky Register* (Sandusky, Ohio), November 29, 1955
[3] Overfield, Joseph M. *Easter's Charisma, Remarkable Slugging Captivated Fans*. Published 1984, accessed through Research.SABR.org.
[4] Ibid.
[5] Ibid.
[6] *The Coshocton Democrat* (Coshocton, Ohio), January 27, 1956
[7] Overfield
[8] *Long Beach Independent* (Long Beach, California), February 28, 1956
[9] Wancho, Joseph, Rick Huhn, Leonard Levin, Bill Nowlin, and Steve Johnson. *Pitching to the Pennant: The 1954 Cleveland Indians*. (Lincoln: The University of Nebraska Press, 2014), Pg. 181
[10] Stadium history accessed through milb.com
[11] *Warren Times Mirror* (Warren, Pennsylvania), April 2, 1956
[12] *Miami News* (Miami, Florida), April 3, 1956
[13] *Miami News* (Miami, Florida), April 18, 1956
[14] *Miami News* (Miami, Florida), May 4, 1956
[15] *The Gazette* (Montreal, Canada), May 8, 1956
[16] *Democrat and Chronicle* (Rochester, New York), May 1, 1957
[17] *Democrat and Chronicle* (Rochester, New York), May 18, 1956
[18] *Newark Advocate* (Newark, Ohio), May 30, 1956

[19] *The Terre Haute Tribune* (Terre Haute, Indiana), Jun 15, 1956
[20] *The Austin American* (Austin, Texas), June 3, 1956
[21] *Pittsburgh Courier*, June 9, 1955
[22] *Democrat and Chronicle* (Rochester, New York), July 14, 1956
[23] Russert, Tim. *Big Russ & Me: Father & Son: Lessons of Life.* (New York: Hachette Books, 2014).
[24] Russert
[25] *Democrat and Chronicle* (Rochester, New York), August 6, 1956
[26] Overfield
[27] *Shamokin News-Dispatch* (Shamokin, Pennsylvania), December 27, 1956
[28] Wancho, 181
[29] Figures accessed through milb.com
[30] *Indianapolis News,* May 22, 1957
[31] *The Sheboygan Press* (Sheboygan, Wisconsin), June 13, 1957
[32] Overfield
[33] Wancho, 181
[34] Ibid.
[35] Russert
[36] *Democrat and Chronicle* (Rochester, New York), July 26, 1957
[37] *Elmira Advertiser* (Elmira, New York), September 9, 1957
[38] Standings accessed through BaseballReference.com
[39] *Democrat and Chronicle* (Rochester, New York), September 12, 1957
[40] *Democrat and Chronicle* (Rochester, New York), September 17, 1957
[41] Zygner, Sam. *The Forgotten Marlins: A Tribute to the 1956-1960 Original Miami Marlins.* (Lanham: The Scarecrow Press, 2013), Pg. 122
[42] Ibid., 200
[43] *Democrat and Chronicle* (Rochester, New York), September 22, 1957
[44] Overfield
[45] Ibid.
[46] *Buffalo Courier-Express,* May 14, 1959
[47] Wancho, 182
[48] Tygiel, 260
[49] Posanski
[50] Wancho, 182
[51] *Atlanta Constitution*, April 5, 1969
[52] Manelaro, Jim, and Scott Pitoniak. *Silver Seasons: The Story of the Rochester Red Wings* (Syracuse: Syracuse University Press, 1996), Pg.117
[53] Tygiel, 260
[54] Wancho, 182
[55] Tygiel, 260
[56] *Des Moines Tribune*, May 8, 1964
[57] *The Post-Standard* (Syracuse, New York), November 4, 1965
[58] Wancho, 182
[59] *The Paducah Sun* (Paducah, Kentucky), February 14, 1969
[60] *Clarion-Ledger* (Jackson, Mississippi), July 22, 1969
[61] Ibid.
[62] *Akron Beacon Journal*, February 14, 1969

[63] Ibid.
[64] *The Daily Times* (Salisbury, Maryland), June 17, 1970
[65] *Arizona Republic* (Phoenix, Arizona), July 14, 1973

**'Conclusion' Notes**

[1] *Newark Advocate* (Newark, Ohio), March 30, 1979
[2] Wancho, 182
[3] Simkus, 261
[4] Ibid.
[5] *Akron Beacon Journal,* March 30, 1979
[6] *Cleveland Plain Dealer,* April 4, 1979
[7] Ibid.
[8] Wancho, 183
[9] *Daily News* (New York, New York), April 1, 1979
[10] *Akron Beacon Journal,* March 30, 1979
[11] Lebovitz, 70
[12] *Cleveland Plain Dealer,* April 11, 1979
[13] Ibid.
[14] *Democrat and Chronicle* (Rochester, New York), April 22, 1979

**'Appendix A' Notes**

[1] Wancho, 178
[2] *Honolulu Star-Bulletin,* September 21, 1946
[3] *Collier's*, August 5, 1950
[4] McNeil, William F. *Black Baseball Out of Season: Pay for Play Outside the Negro Leagues.* Jefferson, McFarland and Company, 2007. Pg. 171
[5] *Collier's*, August 5, 1950
[6] Murphy
[7] Murphy
[8] *The Coshocton Democrat* (Coshocton, Ohio), January 27, 1956

Made in the USA  
San Bernardino, CA  
28 December 2018